Outdoor Art for Kids

Outdoor Art
for Kids

written and illustrated by
CHARLEEN KINSER

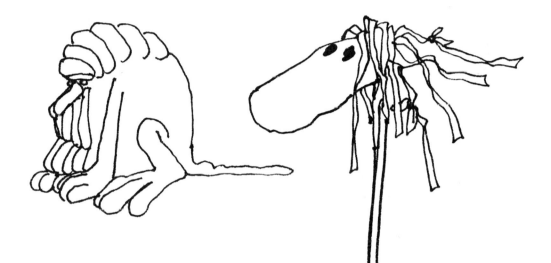

FOLLETT PUBLISHING COMPANY
Chicago

ISBN 0–695–40533–0 Titan binding
ISBN 0–695–80533–9 Trade binding

Library of Congress Catalog Card Number: 74–18133

First Printing

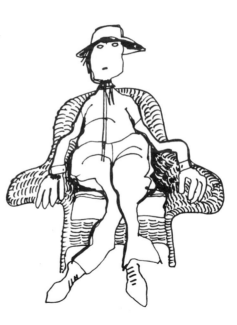

11/75

To Thomas and Maggie Ellyn,

who gave me all

the beautiful gifts

of their sandbox

years.

Contents

Thanks

My thanks to the young artists who designed and produced the artwork for the photographs in this book:

Larry Coburn
Sonya Fischer
Kevin, Bryan, and Karen Gill
Thomas and Maggie Kinser
Erin, Michael, Jennifer, Richard, Mark,
    Maureen, and Aileen Quan
Kelly Rupe
Sue and Janet Sterkel
Annette Toews
Richard Van Etta

Introduction

There are times when you want to be outdoors just because—because the rain has just made a river of your street or you want to make the first boot tracks in the snow. Maybe there's a game of street ball getting started or a road crew at work—with a tar pot. Or you want to turn orange with everything else in the late sun.

Then there are times when someone—maybe your mother—says, "Why don't you go outdoors for a while?" Those are usually the times when there's nothing to do out there.

Take this book and go. There are some great things to make outdoors almost all the time. Things you can have fun trying and tinkering with and finding out about—all alone or with friends. Making things outdoors is great, since you don't have to be careful of this and careful of that or worry about being neat. And outdoors is very big. That means you can make very big things if you feel like it.

Just what sorts of things you can make depends mostly on where your outdoors is and what kind of weather goes with it. It depends, too, on what you think would be really fun to make, and of course, how big you are and whether you have a few friends to help.

I've discovered that no one is more inventive than a kid who wants to make something. Young people like you de-

signed and made the things in the photographs in this book. The diagrams that show how they made their things are shared here to give you ideas—to nudge your inventiveness so you will have as much fun as they did luring the wind into play, constructing an ice castle, finding eerie musical sounds, or trying to turn a monster into stone.

Certain materials and one kind of tool or another are needed to make most things—even outdoors. The materials and tools you can find to use will help you decide just what you can make. A list of places to look for the less common materials and tools mentioned in this book follows each group of projects.

Tools can be dangerous if used wrongly, so ask someone who might know how to use the tools you borrow. And take time to read the directions and cautions on the labels of materials such as glues, paints, acrylic sprays, and plasters. Being careful of yourself is part of being a craftsman.

Now, why don't you go outdoors and make something fantastic?

Nothing Very Exciting Ever Happens in a Backyard?

One

Suppose one midsummer morning you wake before the sun's fingers find their way to your window. The air is cool, and just a trickle of pink squeezes through the thin, gray sky, and you squint back at it over the covers. A very strange feeling comes over you. There's something different about this particular morning. You dress in a hurry and go quietly out to meet it.

The ground is still wet and cool from the night. There's the sticky strand of morning web across the walk—an ingenious spider's breakfast trap. As you brush it from your face, it occurs to you suddenly that you are not alone. For a while you go on walking, trying to whistle a little, as if having company wouldn't bother you a bit.

Finally, no longer able to resist, you stop and slide your eyes slowly sideways. And there, standing quite still, something very big is watching you.

It's an effigy. It looks kind of real, like a person or a beast, but you know better. You made it and planted it there yesterday. It's scary even though you knew it was there all along. But what will it do to the kid down the street when he wanders by? It'll scare him stiff—as stiff as another beast-thing standing there.

Effigies

An effigy seems to come to mind one part at a time. Whichever part comes to your mind first is the part to make first. Most effigies eventually have these four basic parts.

Head, or two
Skeleton (whatever holds it up)
Appendages (a fancy name for arms, hands, legs, tails). Some effigies wear feet, but if an effigy travels at all it is carried, or maybe pulled in a wagon.
Skin or covering (such as clothing)

To introduce you to the great variety of effigies, here is a catalog of parts and their simple beginnings.

Heads

(1) Old pillowcase stuffed with newspapers, rags, dried grasses, or straw. It may be coated with gesso to make it stiff and weatherproof.

Gesso is a white painting ground that dries hard. It is used by artists to make a firm, waterproof surface for painting. All cloth, paper, cardboard, or straw parts of effigies may be coated with gesso to make them stiff and waterproof. Paint it on and wait about half an hour. When dry, gesso may be covered with paint, dyes, or crayon.

(2) Heavyweight large paper sack stuffed with newspapers, rags, or dried grasses; **(3)** newspaper wads wrapped with strips of cloth (like a mummy).

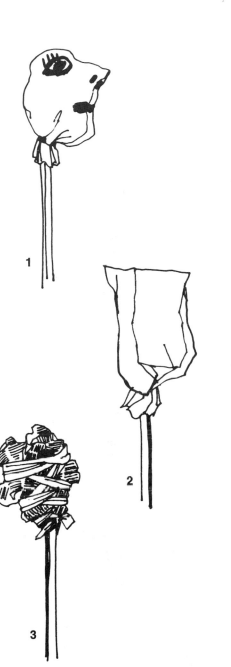

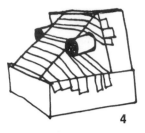

(4) Small corrugated cardboard boxes glued together. Use an all-purpose white glue that will dry quickly and be water-proof. It's a good idea to read the directions on the label before you use any glue.

(5) Empty plastic gallon jug. Here the mouth is a hole cut in the jug, and the nose is the handle. *Be careful, though. Plastic jugs often contain laundry bleach and other poisonous liquids. Be sure yours is washed out before you work with it.*

Effigy hair is always a mess. It might be **(6)** an old string mop, **(7)** a wrapped

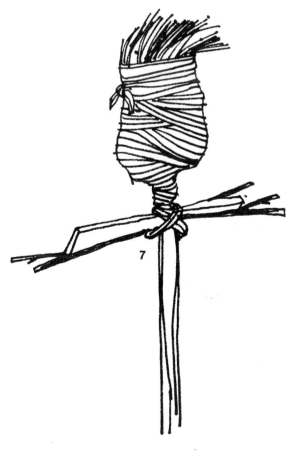

broom, **(8)** grasses tied in bunches, **(9)** corn shucks, **(10)** excelsior (a wood shaving packing material), **(11)** torn strips of rags, or tangles of string or yarn.

8

9

10

11

An effigy nose might be **(12)** a paper wad (lumpy), **(13)** a corncob (rough), a stick (pointy), a cardboard tube, **(14)** a paper cup, a tin can, **(15)** a stuffed sock, or **(16)** an old potato (wrinkly).

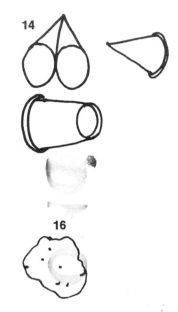

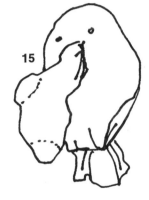

(17) Effigy eyes are not always a matched pair. Some are just empty holes or flat, painted-on starey things. They may be bright and shiny tin can lids or bicycle reflectors (very startling), popped-out eyes of frozen juice cans, or various beads or balls.

Ears are not always found on effigies but are sometimes cut from cardboard, tufts of straw, old socks, **(18)** rubber gloves, or **(19)** large, leathery leaves.

Fangs and horns or antlers are sometimes found on effigies and might be **(20)** sticks, twigs, or **(21)** cones of paper.

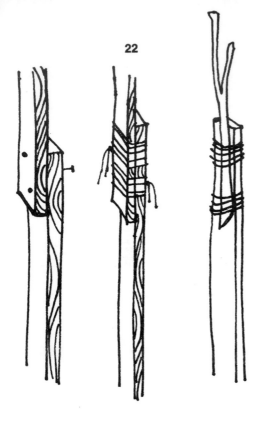

22

Skeletons

A very tall effigy must have a very tall (long) backbone. The backbone may be in one piece, but more often it is made up of shorter pieces joined together with nails, or all-purpose white glue and heavy cord, in one of these ways **(22)**.

Any kind of string that is strong enough to hold the various parts of an effigy together may be used. Kite string, heavy package cord, jute cord, or even shoelaces may do the job.

The simplest knot, and the one most often found on effigies, is the square knot (see page 50). It is easy to tie and won't slip.

The most common kind of skeleton is the long cross, made in one of these ways **(23)**.

23

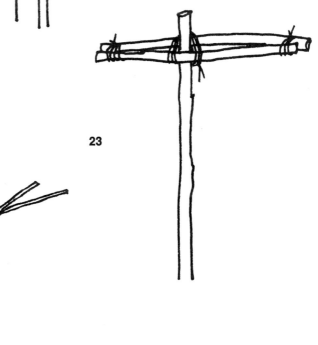

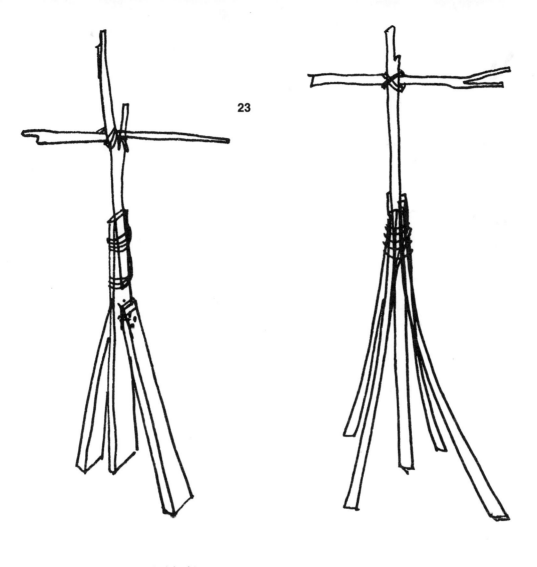

23

This **(24)** is one way to bind two crossing sticks together before tying a square knot.

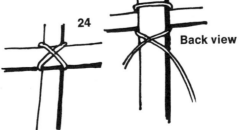

24

Back view

19

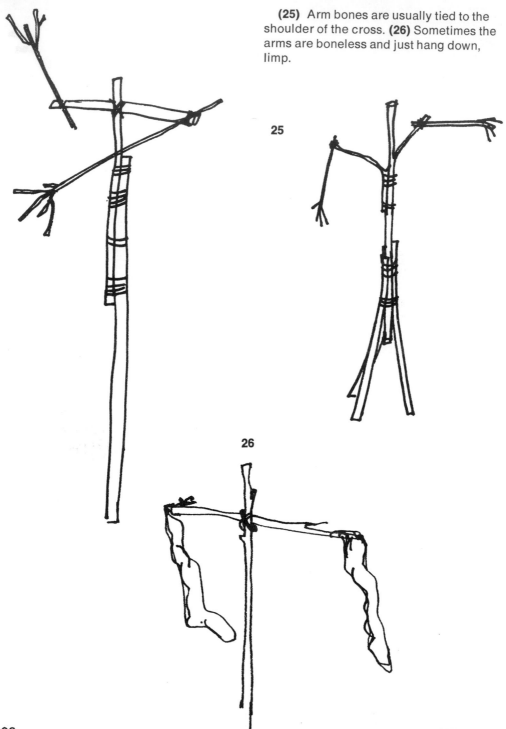

(25) Arm bones are usually tied to the shoulder of the cross. **(26)** Sometimes the arms are boneless and just hang down, limp.

25

26

(27) The shortie effigy is held up by a tree stump or trash can.

(28) A natural resting-place for dragon-like effigies is an iron or wood picket fence.

(29) A similar skeleton for dragon-beasts is a row of short and tall crosses. As you see, the tip-top of each cross is one bump in the backbone and the shorter, crossing stick of each cross is a rib or a hipbone.

27

28

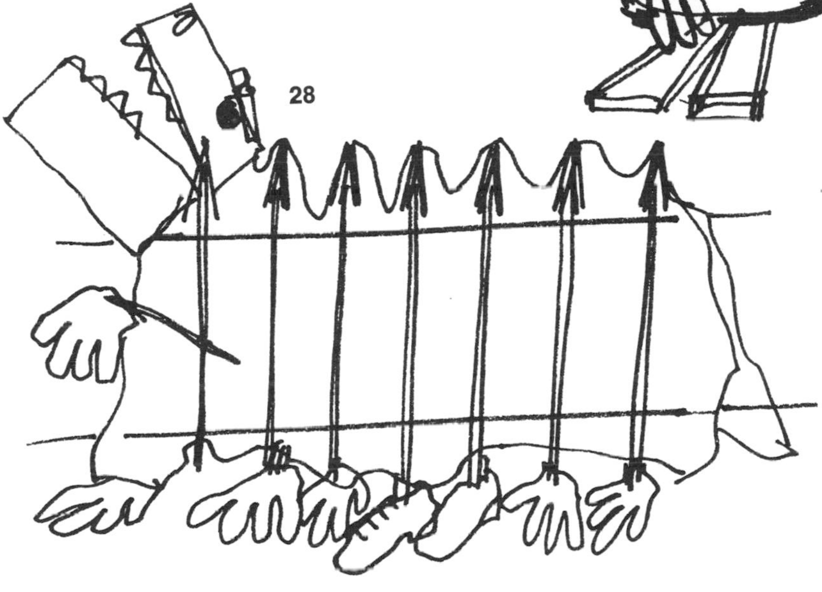

29

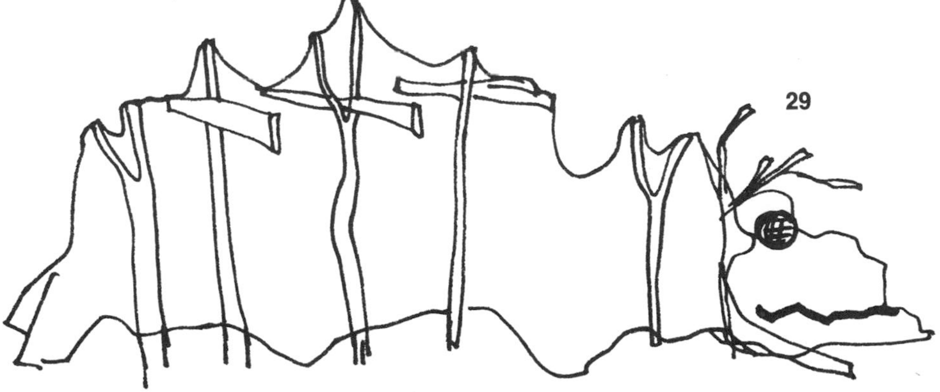

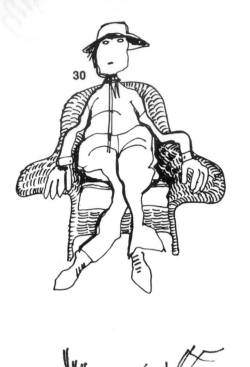

30

(30) The porch effigy is a spineless collection of stuffed clothes and is usually slumped in a chair with only a neck bone to hold up its head.

(31) Those with clothesline-pole skeletons sometimes come in pairs and occasionally have feet—even though they do not travel. **(32)** Another kind of clothesline figure has many arms.

(33) Wood or chain-link-fence effigies have arms and a neck bone to hold up their heads. They, too, are often exceptions to the no-feet rule. But the feet are purely ornamental.

31

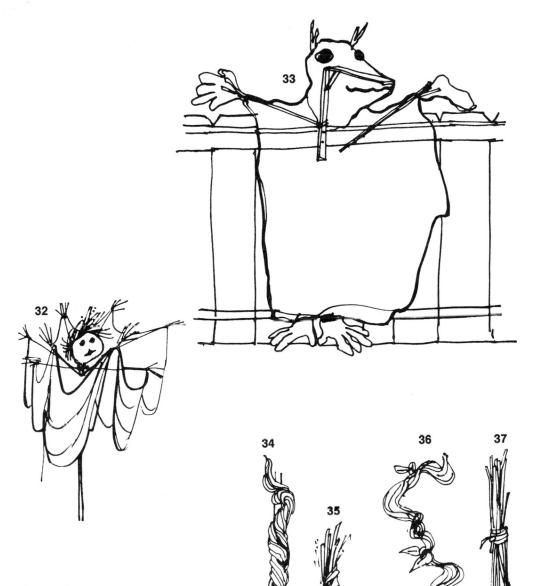

Appendages

Arms and legs and tails seem to get all
mixed up on effigies. What is a tail on one
is an arm or two or three on another: **(34)**
stick wrapped with rags and coated with
gesso; **(35)** straw or grasses tied to sticks;
(36) twisted newspapers or rags wrapped
around wire and coated with gesso; **(37)**
bundle of long sticks tied here and there;

(38, 39) pants legs and shirt-sleeves stuffed with newspapers, rags, grasses, or even inflated balloons to make them fat.

Effigies usually have either pretty ridiculous-looking paws of stuffed socks, or lumpy-fingered hands of rubber or garden gloves (rarely matching), or wispy brooms of grasses, or terrible, clawlike rakes of twigs.

They sometimes wear somebody else's shoes for feet, or have feet flat as boards (which they are), or stand around in stuffed socks.

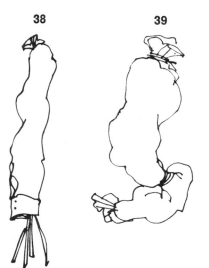

38　　　　**39**

Skin

Effigy skin is rarely tight-fitting but hangs and bags loosely around the skeleton. It may or may not be stuffed, but if stuffed fat, the effigy is usually nice and lumpy. The skin might be a discarded sheet, rags of all sorts, or old clothes in large sizes. It may even be very scratchy dried grasses or straw tied directly to the skeleton. Sometimes a straw or newspaper covering is dressed with old stockings slipped over it or rag strips wrapped around it. A gesso coating gives a very crusty appearance.

The finishing touches may be a great hat or crown or a string of trinkets such as an effigy might wear to rattle in the wind. Try adding something to glimmer in the sun or moonlight and bright paper strips or cloth sashes. Effigies have also been known to wear chains, necklaces of tin cans, bells, gourds, pinecones, flowers, doll heads, and other mystery-bearing junk.

When an effigy appears suddenly in a neighborhood, it sometimes attracts others within the week.

Sources for Materials

Gesso—artists' supply stores and some craft shops

Excelsior—ask in housewares departments and import shops for a bagful from shipped items they receive

Jute cord—hardware, drug, variety stores; craft and hobby shops

Wood scraps—scrap bins at lumber yards, discards from stores that receive crated items, old mop and broom handles

Turned to Stone

Two

There was once a surly little creature who wanted to be famous more than anything; and because of his fierceness, not to mention his gross appearance, he was accustomed to having his own way. He traveled a well-worn path to a small kingdom where, by his mischief-making, he quickly became a terror. One morning, without so much as a "Good day, your highness," the wretched creature ate the king and moved into the palace. He called himself Terrible Algernon.

Since this kingdom lay on a path often traveled by beasts on their way from somewhere to somewhere else, the coming of Algernon was not its first catastrophe. The tower bells rang the alert. The town council went once again to a cliff by the sea, where lived a wizard with certain awesome powers, and brought the matter to his attention.

"Yes, yes, I know; another fame-seeking creature," sighed the waspish old wizard. He swirled into his cloak and went to the creature king in a most deceptive manner of friendliness.

The wizard bowed low and poured his words like syrup: "I am Master Wizard, and creator of statues."

"Aagh!" snorted Algernon, eyeing the wizard narrowly. "Where, then, is *my* statue?" His voice sent a tremor through the palace. "A shabby lion guards my steps, a ridiculous man-warrior marks the town square, gargoyles grin from their rain gutters, and fat, stupid cupids occupy the fountains," and he frothed a little at the thought. "*I* must be a statue," he screamed, scrambling to the top of the throne, "in some very special place."

"By all means you shall be," chimed the wizard. "Why, just today a group of your subjects came to me with a similar idea. And the place for your statue is our most special—Immortal Island in the great Self Sea—reserved for the likes of you."

Then, with a great flapping of his cloak, the wizard mumbled: *"Sic semper tyrannis. Finis coronat opus."* ("Thus always to tyrants. The end crowns the work.")

"Enough of your fluttering and muttering, old fool," snapped Algernon uneasily. "Where is my statue?"

He stomped his foot; it came down with unusual heaviness.

"It is begun," soothed the wizard. "My private oarsmen are waiting even now to row you to Immortal Island."

The people of the kingdom cheered at the cliff's edge as their creature king was lowered royally to the wizard's rowboat. But Algernon heard only faintly now, and he was uncomfortably stiff. He sat erect and motionless, like a prow ornament taking a boat ride. Soon all was quiet but the rhythmic oars.

When the boat beached, Terrible Algernon's sight was dim; but he saw vague, still figures before him on the shore. The oarsmen unloaded him, rather unroyally, and placed him alongside many statues. That final, stiffening realization would last forever: he, Terrible Algernon, had been turned to stone.

Sand Casting

Turning something to stone is indeed an awesome talent, but doing it without magical powers is nearly as exciting.

You'll need: wet sand about 12″ deep (in a sandbox or at the beach); water to keep it wet (a garden hose with a spray nozzle, or a sprinkling can with tiny holes); plaster of paris (for small statues) and a pail or can for mixing it; or plaster and sand mix (for large statues) and a pail or wagon for mixing them.

Plaster of paris is fine for small statues. It sets up (hardens) in 15 minutes, faster if mixed with seawater, and dries completely within an hour. You can make the finished statue weatherproof with acrylic spray or shellac.

A half-and-half combination of plaster mix and sand mix (which contains cement) will make a less brittle, more weatherproof statue and is recommended for creatures more than 12″ tall. It will dry in less than a day.

To create a stone statue you must first imagine a creature lying face down in the wet sand, making an impression where it lies **(40)**. That impression will become the mold for your statue. Of course, you must dig out its shapes yourself, and that requires a sort of inside-out thinking. Whatever is to stick out on the statue (nose, tusks, toes, belly) will be a hole in the sand mold. Whatever is to be a hole in the statue (mouth, deep eyes, dents) will be a bump in the mold **(41)**.

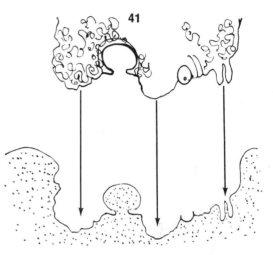

41

40

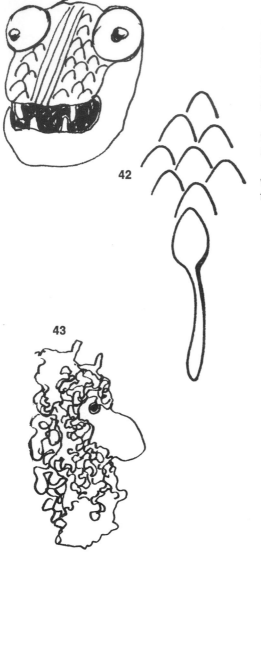

Make the walls around the mold thick and high enough to hold the plaster mixture you'll pour into it to turn the invisible creature into stone. Your hands are the only tools you'll need to make most details, but a stick is handy for little bumps. A spoon makes a nice scaly texture **(42)**.

Dribble very wet sand for a squiggly texture **(43)**—good for hair and beards and wrinkly skin.

Your statue will be flat in back, but it will stand alone if you give it big, flat feet **(44)**.

42

43

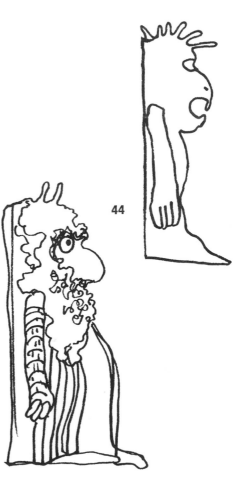

44

To make an open and toothsome mouth
(45), approach the sand as if you were
going to scoop up a double handful.
Scoop deep into the sand until you sense
that your fingers are about to meet (46).
The near-tunnels made by your fingers
will become the teeth. The mound made
by your cupped hands will be the open
mouth.

Shells and cones, seeds, marbles, and
such may be stuck into the mold. Remember, what faces down in the mold will face
outward in the finished statue.

45

When your mold is ready to fill, mix only
as much plaster of paris or plaster and
sand mix as you think you will use at one
time. You'll have to guess at the amount
as you mix it, looking at the size of your
mold.

Pour the dry mix into a wagon bed or a
pail and add water, stirring with your
hands until it is the consistency of cake
batter or thin paste.

For best results with details, spatter the
plaster mixture with your hands into the
details first, then pour it or scoop it with a
coffee can to fill the mold halfway.

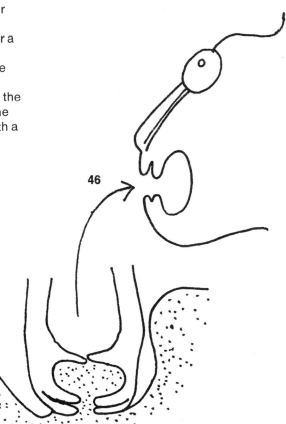

46

To make the statue stronger, add sticks, long, dry weeds, or a flat piece of chicken wire before pouring in the rest of the plaster mixture **(47)**.

If your statue is small and is to hang on a wall, you must put a loop of heavy wire, knotted cord, or some other hanger in its back while the mixture is still wet **(48)**.

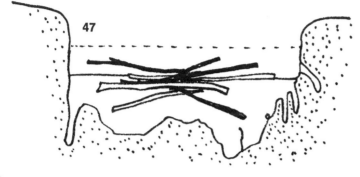

47

48

When your statue is hard and dry to the touch it is ready to lift out of the mold. Dig the sand away from the edges and raise the statue to a standing position. Prop it up so the molded front surface can dry for a few more hours in the sun or warm air. The loose sand sticking to the molded surface may be brushed off with an old scrub brush, broom, or rag—or, if the statue is made of plaster and sand mix, it can be rinsed off with a quick spray of water.

Sources for Materials

Sand for a sandbox—try builders' supply stores, or call your city parks department and ask for a source

Plaster of paris—hardware stores, craft and hobby shops, artists' supply stores

Plaster mix—hardware and builders' supply stores, lumberyards

Sand mix—same as for Plaster mix

Acrylic spray—hardware, artists' supply, or paint stores; paint and art supply departments; craft and hobby shops

Shellac—paint and hardware stores and departments

Cages and Webs   Three

Olac, a weaver of baskets, journeyed far gathering oak and willow twigs for his craft. As shadows lengthened, he piled the sticks high on his back and started for home. Along the way he stopped by a stream to pick reeds, when a snarl of trolls sprang out before him.

Thinking quickly to save his life, Olac gasped, "At last! You must be the mad weavers to whom I bring these terrible, enchanted sticks."

He staggered a bit under his load, feigning its mastery over him. The ugly trolls backed away cautiously.

"They have ridden me as if I were a beast of burden," Olac complained. "Made me carry them piggyback these many miles from Ekbacken."

The twisted little men muttered among themselves, and keeping their distance for the moment, held Olac at bay with their eyes.

Calmly, Olac put down his load, chose a number of long twigs, and began weaving. The trolls shuffled closer to watch. "Hear me well if you are to master these wicked sticks," he said, "for I am to show the secret only once."

Olac's spidery fingers were at home in the web of sticks, and he chanted words from his craft, which he hoped would sound magical to the wretched little men:

Slype the withes and pair them so,
Around the spokes the weavers go.
Add the stakes of chestnut spale,
And for the upsett, four-rod wale.
Scallom to an ozier ring,
And rand the rounds to shape the thing.

The trolls were dazzled. The powerful sticks had yielded to the mysterious words and bent to the stranger's will.

"Now you must do as I have done," warned Olac. "Weave all the sticks before dawn, for those left unwoven will beat you unmercifully."

The eager trolls thrashed about, wrestling the enchanted sticks and muttering Olac's words as best they could. And clever Olac left them to their task. Like a phantom reed, he wove his path through the trees, homeward.

Weaving

Here are the meanings of Olac's mysterious words:

   Slype—a slanting cut made to thin the ends of twigs
   Withes—another name for willow twigs
   Pair—pairing is a weave using two weavers
   Spokes—the foundation sticks of a basket base
   Weavers—twigs or other materials woven around the spokes and stakes
   Stakes—the foundation sticks for the sides of a basket
   Spale—thin strips of wood that can be used as weavers or stakes
   Upsett—setting up the basket sides to begin its shape
   Rod—another name for twig
   Four-rod wale—a four-rod weave often used in the upsett
   Scallom—to fasten stakes to a ring to hold them upright
   Ozier—another name for willow
   Rand—randing is a single-rod weave (over one, under one)
   Rounds—rows of weaving

Olac's chant describes the making of an elaborate basket. But you don't have to be a master basketmaker to make wonderful woven things with twigs or yarns. You can weave a simple roll-up bed (page 41), a fence or hut (page 42), an Ojo de Dios (page 42), or a whimsical hat (page 41). Of course, your fingers have to learn to do what you want them to do, so each piece of weaving you try helps make the next piece easier and more beautiful.

   Try out your fingers with a fanciful web among the twigs of a large branch. There are no rules and no maps any better than the ones you invent in your own mind and work out with your own efforts.

   Find a branch with something special about it and make it even more special with your meandering yarns or string or fishing line. The knots on pages 49–51 may be useful for attaching the foundation threads (or warp threads, as cloth weavers call them) to the branches. You may wrap your yarn or string on sticks or cardboard bobbins **(49)** to make it

49

easier to handle while you weave. Try a variety of colors and textures and some of the weaves on pages 35-36. Entrap your most special finds—a peacock feather, a sea shell, or the spidery head of Queen Anne's lace—in the weaves of your web.

Basketry is the name given to weaving when twigs, bark, roots, vines, and grasses are used as weavers instead of yarns or cords. Any long strong leaves, flexible woody stems or shoots may be used in basketry. Some really good plant materials to look for are honeysuckle, ivy, and clematis vines; coralberry runners; palm, day lily and cattail leaves; hazelnut, poplar, weeping and other willow shoots; willow bark; and maidenhair fern stems.

Most vines and grasses may be cut in any season and dried for use later. But shoots or twigs are best picked from late autumn, when the leaves fall, until the sap rises in the spring.

50

Strip off any remaining leaves and remove the bark if you wish. The bark will peel off very easily if you can boil the twigs for several hours. Otherwise, carefully cut lengthwise through the outer and inner bark on opposite sides of the shoots and peel off the bark slowly **(50)**. The bark may also be used as weavers. Dry the shoots and bark in a shady, airy place.

You may use green shoots and leaves to try out weaves and to make temporary hats, mats, or baskets, but fresh shoots and leaves shrink as they dry out, causing gaps in the weaving.

Before weaving with dried shoots, vines, leaves, or strips of peeled bark, soak them for 15 to 30 minutes in cool water (in a pail, a washtub, a big puddle, or a bathtub) to make them flexible. Remove the soaked weavers and wrap them in a damp cloth to allow them to "mellow," as basketmakers say. They will be even easier to weave with after 10 minutes of mellowing.

Whether you weave with twigs or yarns, these basic weaves are good to know.

Randing **(51)**—a simple, over one, under one weave to be worked over an uneven number of stakes. The ends of old and new weavers lie behind the same stake.

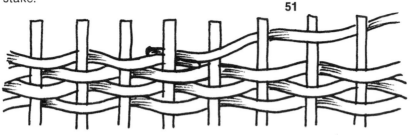

51

Rib-randing **(52)**—an over two, under one weave to be worked over any number of stakes not divisible by three. The ends of old and new weavers lie behind the same stake.

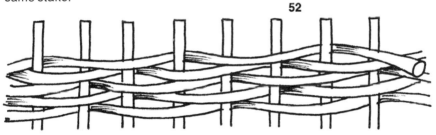

52

Pairing **(53,54)**—begin by doubling a weaver around a stake to make two weavers of it. End old weavers behind two different stakes. Add two new weavers behind those same two stakes **(55)**.

53

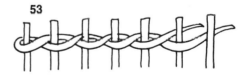

54

Top view   **55**

Chasing **(56)**—randing with two weavers over an even number of stakes. End old and new weavers as in pairing.

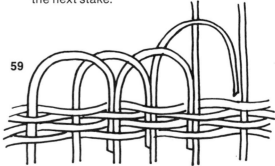

Here are two good borders for twig-weaving or basketry.

Simple trac border **(57, 58)**—the last few inches of the stakes are used as weavers. Weave one stake at a time (over one, under one) until each is woven among the others and ended behind the fourth stake to its right.

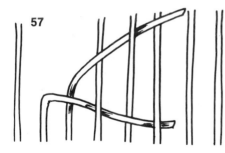

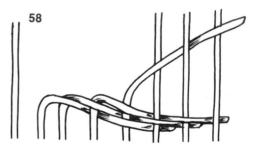

Simple scallop border **(59)**—each stake is bent into an arch in front of one stake and down into the weave alongside the next stake.

The drawings represent basket weaving (working from bottom to top of a basket). If you are making a hat (working from crown to brim, or top to bottom), place a mirror at the top of the drawings. The mirrored image will show how your work should look.

If you are left-handed, place a mirror at the right of the drawings. The mirrored image will show how your right-to-left work will look.

If you are left-handed and making a hat (working from crown to brim), turn the drawings upside-down.

When weaving with yarns, cord, or raffia, new weavers must be tied to the ends of the old weavers (see knots on pages 49–51). But in twig weaving the pressure of the weavers against the spokes and stakes holds all the twigs in place. To start a weaver, simply place one end behind a spoke (on the inside of a basket, or the back side of a mat) and begin weaving. Hold the weaver in place with your fingers or a spring type clothespin while making the first few strokes of your weave **(60)**. After that the weaver will be held in place by its own pressure against the spokes. Weavers are also ended behind a spoke or stake.

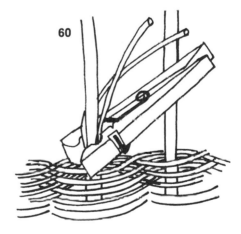

60

As the rounds are woven, pack the weavers tightly against one another to make the weaving firm and even-textured.

You might make a round ornament to try out the beginnings of a basket or hat. The foundation sticks or spokes must be flexible enough to be bent into a radiating pattern (like wheel spokes). The weavers should be thinner than the foundation sticks, and may be: jute, string, ribbon, yarns; raffia, vines, or other thin basketry materials.

Begin with four or five foundation sticks. They may be green, flexible sticks, but for a nicer piece of weaving use dry sticks that have been soaked in water until flex-

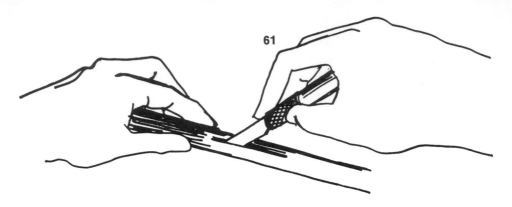

61

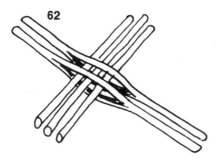

62

ible as described on page 34. *If you can use a knife,* cut slots **(61)** through the centers of two sticks and push the other two or three sticks through the slots **(62).** If you cannot use a knife, or if your foundation sticks are very thin, just cross them **(63).**

Pairing is a good weave to hold the spokes in place (see page 35). Bend a long weaver in half to make two weavers, and slip the loop over two of the spokes. Pair around the four groups of spokes **(64).** Then bend the spokes to make a

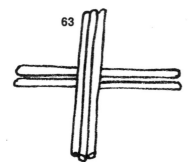

63

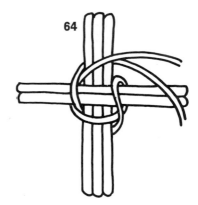

64

radiating pattern as you pair around each individual spoke **(65).**

Pairing with two weavers of different colors over an even number of spokes makes stripes; over an uneven number of spokes, a spiral pattern is made.

If you'd like to use the randing weave in your round ornament, you must add a spoke. After a few rows of pairing, slype a stick **(66)**, and insert it as shown **(67)** to make an uneven number of spokes. Drop one weaver and continue by randing with the other weaver **(68).**

65

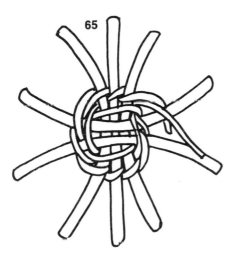

66

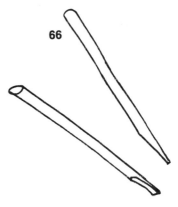

67

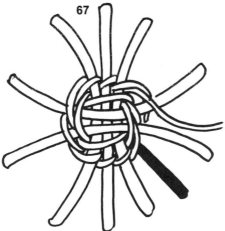

68

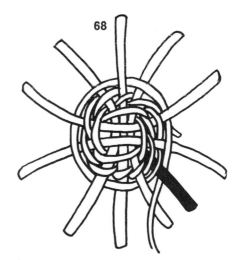

You begin a basket base, a hat crown, or a round mat in the same way a round ornament is started **(61–68)**. The *sides* of a round-bottom basket or a hat are made by bending the spokes upward or downward **(69)**. They are then called stakes. To

69

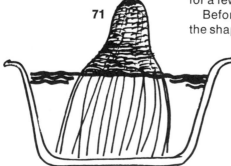

70

71

hold the stakes in place, "Scallom to an ozier ring," says Olac. That is, tie them up with a ring of coathanger wire or cord **(70)**, or use a bowl, pail, tin can, or other form to weave around. You may use two or three different forms to shape one piece of weaving.

A hat or basket is shaped by tightening the weavers to pull the stakes inward or by bending the stakes outward before weaving. The stakes and the twig, leaf, or vine weavers are worked while wet. When they dry, they hold whatever shape they have taken.

To dampen the stakes of a partially woven basket or hat, place it in water so that the unworked stakes are submerged for a few minutes **(71)**.

Before starting a hat or basket, think of the shape and size you'd like your weaving to take. Then use a flexible twig to measure the length the foundation sticks should be, allowing 6″ extra at each end for a finishing border (72).

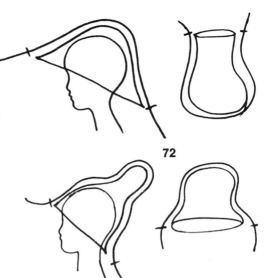

72

The hat in the photograph was made from thin (size 2) commercial reed, but weeping willow rods work nicely for a sturdier hat. The weavers were day lily leaves, pussy willow bark, and raffia, with tiny seedpod twigs from a common weed woven in for decoration. The crown was begun like a basket base with 14 foundation sticks (7 crossed by 7 more—making 28 individual spokes).

After the first few rounds of pairing, another reed spoke was added, as in (67), to make an uneven number (29 spokes). The rest of the hat was woven with randing and rib-randing. It was shaped over a large gourd sometimes called a martin gourd, since it is often used as a birdhouse for purple martins.

A simple trac border (57, 58) made with the last 6 inches of the stakes finished the hat.

If you are an impatient sort of troll and want to make something of twigs without a lot of fuss, try pairing straight sticks together with jute cord (73) to make a Plains Indians' roll-up-and-carry stick bed (74). With very thin sticks you'll have a sun shade or a picnic mat.

Or try the simple *Ojo de Dios* (Eye of God) ornaments (see next page). These are traditionally made by crossing two straight sticks and wrapping bright-colored yarns around them. Sticks from any shrub or tree, wood dowels, pencils, or ice cream sticks will work. Jute, string, raffia, vines, ribbons, or anything long enough may be used with or instead of yarns.

73

74

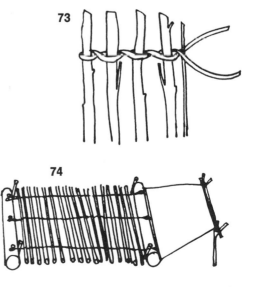

The drawings (75, 76) show the method of wrapping from the front and how it looks from the back. Pull each wrap tight as you make it so there are no gaps between the rows (77). End with a clove hitch (see page 50), hiding the knot ends on the back in the last row of wrapping.

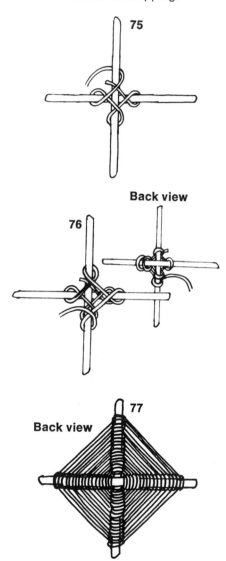

75

76

Back view

Back view

77

A small group of trolls can weave a twig cage or fence in no time at all. Hammer some stakes into the ground and weave thinner sticks among them.

You can weave a hut if you are lucky enough to find some really large tree trimmings. You'll need a pointed stake and a hammer to make holes in the ground for the big foundation branches—or tie them to a porch rail or a fence. Arrange two or three big branches in the hut shape you'd like and weave many of their smaller branches together. Weave in long leaves, thin twigs, strips of cloth, or whatever you can find to make a sturdy, shady meeting place—big enough for two or three sleeping bags, maybe.

You too may believe sticks are enchanted when you begin to work with them.

Sources for Materials

Jute cord—hardware, drug, variety stores; craft and hobby shops

Yarns—yarn shops, needlework departments (usually have some yarns at reduced prices), relatives and friends who knit or weave

Raffia—craft and hobby shops, mail-order craft supply houses (see below)

Basketry reed—same as Raffia

Large tree trimmings—watch for trimmers in your neighborhood, or call your city parks department for a source

Wood dowels—hobby shops, hardware and lumber stores

Mail order craft supply houses— Sax Arts and Crafts
207 North Milwaukee Street
Milwaukee, Wisconsin 53202

The H. H. Perkins Company
10 South Bradley Road
Woodbridge, Connecticut 06525

The Grass Cat   Four

Having looked in every caldron and poked in every cobwebbed corner and reversed every spell she could remember, Wilda resorted to the old "kitty, kitty, kitty" routine. But it was no use. Where in this world, or the next, could she have put that cat? she wondered. She was just hopelessly forgetful—a laughingstock among witches.

On such a stormy night as this, she would surely have company, and if word got around that she'd misplaced her cat again, well, how could she face the others? So she made a cat of twigs and grasses, with marble eyes and thorns for claws, and blackened it all over with soot. Wilda tried hard to think of a spell for turning it into a real cat; but Prince-into-Frog seemed to be all she could remember, and she didn't need a frog.

Lightning flashed, and what seemed to be the wind spitting ashes back down the chimney was Thora, the most evil—and gossipy—witch of all, dropping in for a visit.

Thora's scratchy voice filled the room, and her sharp eyes followed it into every corner; she was *so* nosy.

"It's a wretched night for brooms!" she screeched as she flung her drenched cat over the chair back and slumped before the fire to dry her own tangles. She had already noticed Wilda's fine black cat in the firelight and began bargaining for it, offering a startling recipe.

"It would take more than an old recipe to get this remarkable cat," Wilda chuckled (not wanting her secret to be found out). "Why, he can sit a broom like he was the other end of it, and nothing frightens him."

Suddenly Thora leaped into the air with a blood-chilling shriek that sent her own cat to the roof beams with the bats, but the sooty cat by the fire sat motionless.

"Impressive!" she hissed. "I'll throw in a new chant and a basket of poisoned apples."

Tempted by the apples, but not wanting to be found out, Wilda snorted: "Warts! I wouldn't give up such a fine feline familiar as old what's-his-name for a tricky tune and a few sleep fruits. Let's just forget it and talk about old times, Thora. You have such a fascinating memory. Do you remember the time when I misplaced that old cat and you, the greatest spell caster of all, turned my scrub brush into one?"

"Yes, yes," Thora snapped. "I should think you would want to forget how stupid you were to lose your cat, dumb Wilda."

"But you, clever Thora. I couldn't forget you that night. Such eloquence, such grace as you whirled, your amethyst eyes glowing in the moonlight. Oh, Thora, would you do that magnificent spell for me now?" she begged. "Please, Thora, do it. Do it!"

"All right, all right, Wilda. I *am* rather superb at that one."

Thora did her spell and Wilda clapped. They said their goodnights, and Thora clambered up the chimney into the night. Wilda flung herself over her favorite rafter to sleep. And the sleek black cat by the fire arched and yawned, and settled himself more comfortably.

Bundled-grass Figures

A bundled-grass figure is a little like a quick sketch in the round—the gesture (action or pose) is more important than the little details. Start with a skeleton structure of sticks that suggests a gesture. Bundle, wrap, and tie various grasses, leaves, and pods to the skeleton and surprise yourself.

If you think about making a cat or something from grasses, leaves, and pods, you're bound to find a lot of things in the plant world that seem eager to become parts of animals. It's a lot like playing "find the hidden animals in the picture"— some are upside down or look like something else, but you'll discover them along roads, in vacant lots, or backyards. And one discovery leads to another. Once you find something like a foot posing as a dried lily stalk, you're on your way.

The same plants don't grow every-
where, but here is a sampling of things to
look for:

(78) Evergreen twigs with their scaly
bark, **(79)** dried corn stalks with roots, and

78

(80) the fibrous brown bases of dead palm leaves (which also can be carved easily).

   (81) Wicked thorns from date palms and

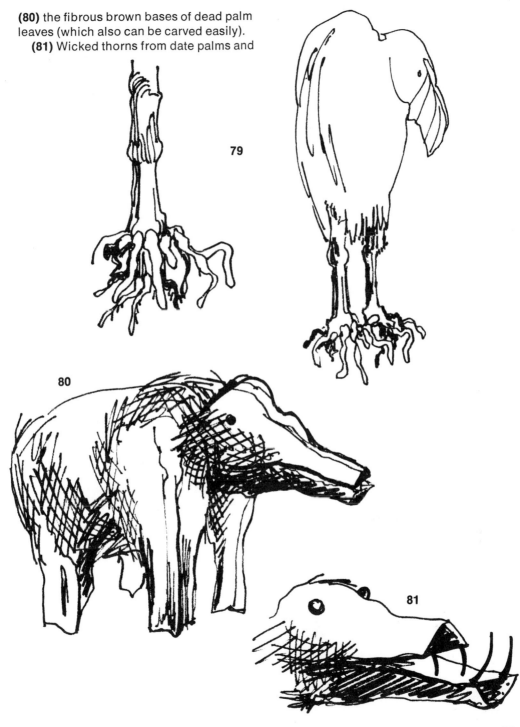

79

80

81

hawthorn, and **(82)** the bayonetlike leaves of yucca. *Treat all thorny plants with great respect, for thorns can hurt you.*

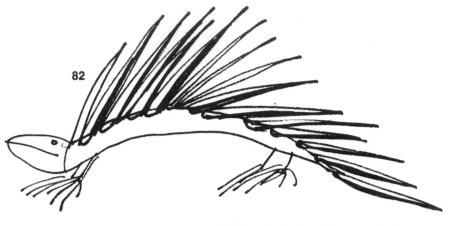

(83) Seeds and pods from such trees as buckeye, eucalyptus, sweetgum, and honey locust.

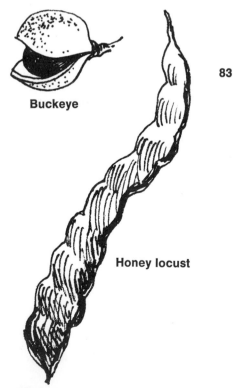

Buckeye

Honey locust

Eucalyptus

Sweetgum

(84) Big, leathery leaves and all sorts of dried weeds, grasses, and grains.

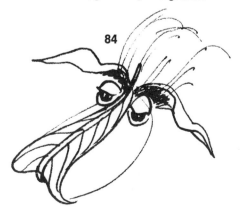

Some of these knots may be useful to you in tying together your skeleton sticks and grass bundles.

Lark's head—form it in your hand **(85)**, then slip it onto a rod, stick, or post **(85a)** and pull both ends tight **(85b)**. This knot also may be formed directly over a rod **(85c, 85d)**.

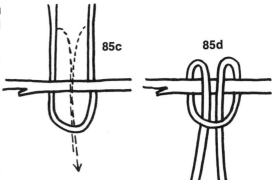

85c

85d

85

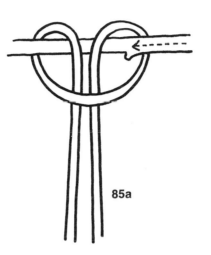

85a

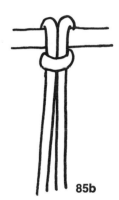

85b

Two half hitches—when tied with one loop over a rod or stick **(86)**, the long end may be pulled taut and the knot slid up tight against the rod.

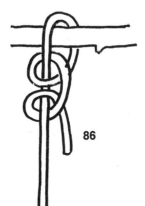

86

87a

Top view

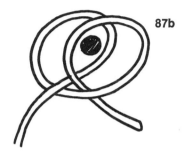

87b

Clove hitch—this is another form of two half hitches. It's good for tying bundles of sticks or grasses. Form it in your hands as loops **(87a, 87b)**, slip it over a rod, and pull both ends taut **(87c)**. Or tie it around a rod or another cord as in **(87d)**.

Square knot—good for tying up bundles and for joining two cords **(88, 88a)**.

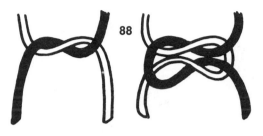

88

Overhand knot—good for tying two or more cords together **(89)**.

87c

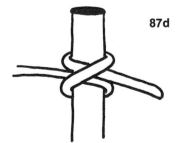

87d

89

Slipping hitch or *overhand noose*—good for pulling a rod end to bend it, or whenever you need a taut cord **(90, 90a)**. Pull the long end of the cord to tighten the noose, and the short end to loosen the noose. You may secure the long end to another rod with a clove hitch **(87d)**.

90

90a

Whipping—a neat, decorative way to wrap many ends together (for a tassel, perhaps) or to tie two or more sticks together side by side **(91)**. Form a loop. Wrap tightly several times with the long end of the cord. Thread the end of the cord through the loop and pull the cord ends tight. The loop disappears under the whipping, holding the cord ends securely. Trim the cord ends close to the whipping.

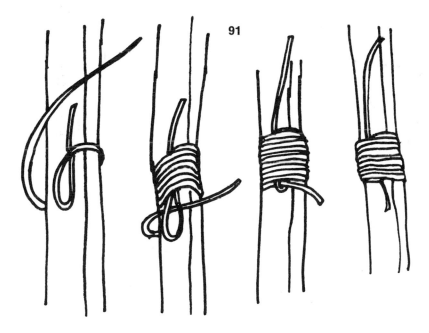

91

This is the way the grass cat in the photograph was made.

(92) Flexible twig bent into an arch and tied with string for the back and upper hind legs.

(93) A forked twig tied in place on the arched back **(92)** for the upper front legs.

(94) Green willow shoots tied at each end of the arched back for ribs.

(95) Dried lily of the Nile flower stalks for legs and feet. The bottoms of the stalks were soaked in water until flexible, then split lengthwise a few inches and wrapped around the forked upper leg twigs.

92

93

94

95

(96) Dried weeds wrapped together to make a long, bushy tail and tied onto the arched back. A grass bundle head tied in place on the arched back twig, and grasses and other weeds tied over ribs and around legs.

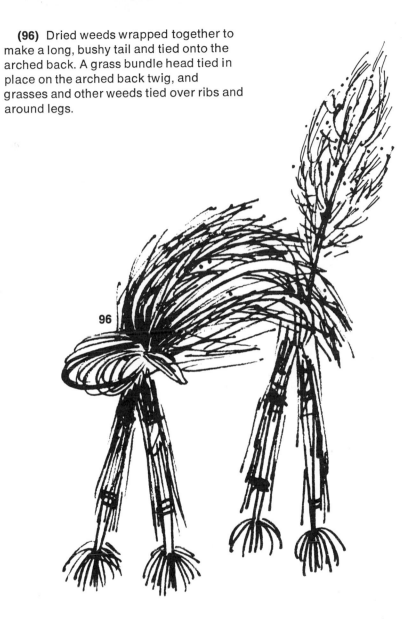

(97) An iris leaf tied over the grass head as a nose. Corn shuck ears and glass bead eyes glued into place.

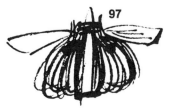

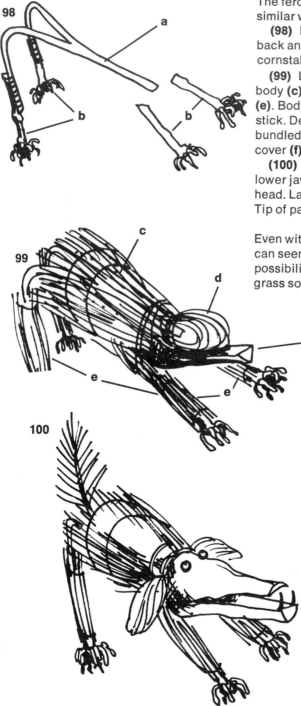

98

a

b

b

The ferocious grass dog was made in a similar way.

(98) Flexible, forked stick **(a)** for the back and upper hind legs. Sawed-off dead cornstalks with roots **(b)** for legs and feet.

(99) Lots of long grasses—bundled for body **(c)** and head **(d)** and to cover legs **(e)**. Body and head bundles tied onto back stick. Dead palm leaf bases tied onto bundled grass head for jaws and head cover **(f)**.

(100) Hawthorn thorn fangs stuck into lower jaw. Wooden bead eyes nailed to head. Large leaves for ears glued to head. Tip of palm leaf for tail stuck into body.

Even without a witch's chant a grass cat can seem to hiss. Don't rule out that possibility until you've made at least one grass something.

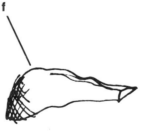

99

c

d

e

e

f

100

54

The Magnificent Lure

Five

O nce, long ago in a village by the sea, a young lad named Lars was in love with a beautiful maiden. He brought her gifts, but she was thankless and always asked for something more. Finally dreaming up an impossible task, she said to him, "Bring me the wind in a silver boat and you may marry me."

Lars was so taken by this thought that he set out at once to find the wind. Not knowing just how to go about it, he went to an old sailor for advice.

The sailor laughed loudly for such an old man. "The winds go their own ways," he said. "Old Boreas blusters down from the north with a heart of ice. Eurus waves sheets of cold from the east. Notus is deceitful; she blows in warm from the south, then tears up trees and beats the shore with 'em. Zephyr, the west wind, is more of a lady—warm and gentle."

"That is the one I must catch," said Lars.

"You'll ne'er catch the wind, m'lad," the old man chuckled, "except as she graces your sails awhile."

But Lars was determined and said, "Then I must entice her to come to me. I will sew a sail of red silk for Zephyr."

And so he began to contrive a lure for the great west wind. He thought of everything he could that ever the wind had shown interest in before. He made windmills, pinwheels, and kites to amuse her; gathered tinkly things to make music, flags to wave, and feathers to flutter. He built a small boat of fine wood and painted it silver. Across the bow he lettered her name: *Zephyr*. Then he waited.

One early summer day he lay back and watched the white clouds. They rolled slowly—out of the west. She was coming. Soon enough, the tallest poplars stirred. It was Zephyr. She drifted down and quizzically skirted the magnificent lure. Slowly at first, with just a puff, she brushed a brightly painted pinwheel and set it whirling. Delighted, she blew harder. The silken sail billowed. Things began to tinkle and whir and spin. Spellbound, Lars inched closer to watch. When he was very near he noticed the scent of clover and heard a sweet old voice whisper his name.

"Larss, Larsss. It's me, Zephyr," and she brushed his cheek. "This is stupendous. I shall spin and dance all summer."

And all summer Lars watched, astonished at the great old wind's agility as she hummed through the maze.

At summer's end Zephyr said to him, "Since you have given me such a splendid gift, I shall return the favor. Board your silver boat, Lars. I shall fill your sail and carry you with me on my journey."

So Lars left his village and sailed with a fair wind on all the seas of the world.

And what of the greedy maiden he left behind? She got her wind—in a boat of silver ice. For when old Boreas came down from the north he crushed the delicate lure trying to make it spin and whirl. He was so enraged by his clumsiness that he stayed there howling forever.

Wind Toys

This maze of amusements for the gentle west wind, Zephyr, is made up of such simple pleasures as pinwheels (page 59), wind flowers and brass flags (this page), a paper wind head (page 58), and (more complicated to make) a two-propeller "thing-a-ma-job" (page 61), a bubble-blowing wind machine (pages 62-63), and a carved pine goose wind finder (pages 64-65).

A charmed wind is a delight to watch at play with things you have designed. Maybe these diagrams and explanations of the magnificent lure in the photograph will be useful to you as you invent your own irresistible amusements for the wind.

Fancy fluted flowers on long, thin stems shimmer and clink, "tinkatinaching."

Punch holes in the centers of little metal kitchen molds (or tiny tin cans) with an awl or hammer and nail, and push thin twigs or wood dowels into the holes. Arrange the stems in the ground so that each flower will clink at least one other when the wind plays among them.

A paper-thin sheet brass flag makes a wonderfully eerie sound and plays with the sunlight as it flutters.

Cut strips in one end of a piece of size 00 or 000 sheet brass. Wrap the other end around a stick and staple it **(101)**. Open up the stapler so that it lies flat. Hold the stick very still, and press the stapler slowly and steadily.

101

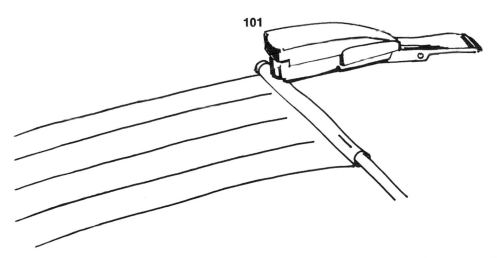

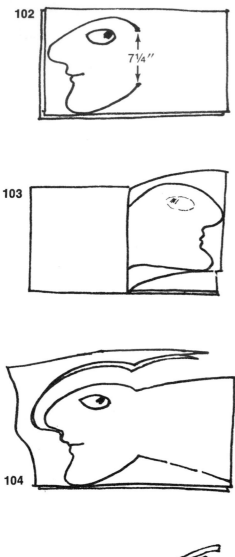

102

7¼"

103

104

The smiling paper head, with strips of hair for the wind to tangle, puffs up and rustles in the wind.

Use two sheets of tissue paper, rice paper, or newspaper. **(102)** Draw a side view of a face with a felt-tipped marker on one half of the top sheet of tissue. Leave a 7¼" blank space at the back of the head. **(103)** Fold back the face half of the top sheet and follow the drawing showing through with a thin line of glue (still leaving the 7¼" space). Fold the top sheet down again to glue it to the bottom sheet.

(104) When the glue is dry, trim both sheets together around the drawing. Turn the papers over to draw the outline and eye on the bottom sheet. Cut hair strips inward toward the center.

Carefully cut the rim from the lid or top of a plastic cottage cheese carton (or make a ring of wire 4¼" across). **(105)** Slip the ring over the hair strips, fold the strips back over the ring (like a cuff), and glue them to it. **(106)** Fasten the head to a wood dowel or stick with string loops.

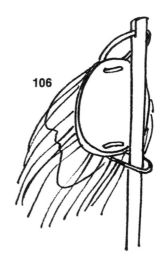

106

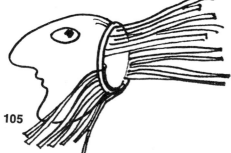

105

The dazzling pinwheel starts out simply and whirls into a colorful blur.

Cut a pinwheel from stiff paper, thin sheet metal, or heavy foil (from a foil pie pan). Try a simple shape first, then see how wild a pinwheel you can make. **(107, 108)** Here are two pinwheel patterns. The second **(108)** is the pattern for the pinwheels in the photograph.

Paint your pinwheel while it is flat. Punch or poke holes (marked by dots) and bend outer (corner) holes together to overlap one another over the center hole. You may glue or staple the over-lapped corners together, leaving the center hole clear.

(109, 109A) Cut a 2″ tube from a plastic drinking straw **(a)** and run an axle **(b)**— bicycle spoke or stiff, thin wire—through the straw and all five holes of the pin-wheel. To keep the pinwheel on the axle, cap a bicycle spoke with a spoke nipple **(c)**. A wire axle may be threaded through and bent over a bead **(d)**.

To mount the pinwheel, cut a thin slot **(e)** with a knife in the end of a stick or dowel and force the axle down into it. A wire axle must be bent downward or wrapped around the stick.

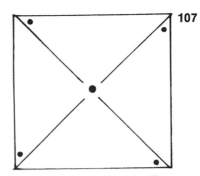

107

Cut along inner and outer lines.

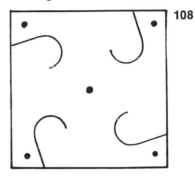

108

109

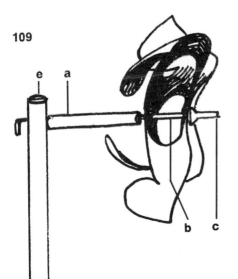

109A

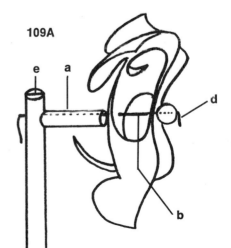

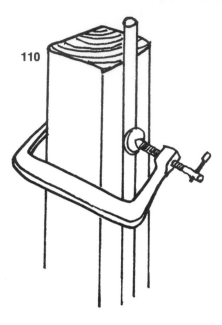

110

Your toys can become more complicated if you can use a drill and a coping saw and you have a vise. You should always use a vise—or substitute—to hold wood while you saw or drill holes. If you don't have a vise, you may be able to attach a C-clamp on a wood step, rail, old chair seat, or similar sturdy place to hold dowels steady for sawing or drilling **(110)**. Try clamping or even tying dowels to some sort of upright post to drill holes in the ends.

You might try this design **(111)**, or your own method, for making a two-propeller "thing-a-ma-job." The propellers are set at opposing 90° angles so they spin in different directions. The tail turns the propellers into the wind.

Here are the materials you'll need:
2 pieces of balsa wood or stiff cardboard
    $\frac{1}{16}$" x 4" x 15" for propeller blades
    and tail
2 Tinker Toy wheels
6 Tinker Toy rods or $\frac{1}{4}$" dowel pieces,
    each $1\frac{1}{4}$" long
$\frac{1}{2}$" x 36" wood dowel cut into three
    pieces—one $2\frac{3}{4}$" long, one $31\frac{3}{4}$" long
    (supporting rod), one $1\frac{1}{2}$" long (tail
    attachment)
metal washer
$\frac{3}{16}$" wood screw $\frac{1}{2}$" long
all-purpose white glue
large thumbtack

The tools you'll find most useful are:
coping saw
vise or C-clamp
drill and $\frac{1}{4}$" drill bit
awl
ruler
knife (to cut balsa wood)
screwdriver

Following the diagram (which shows all the parts ready to put together), make each part of the "thing-a-ma-job," then assemble them.

111

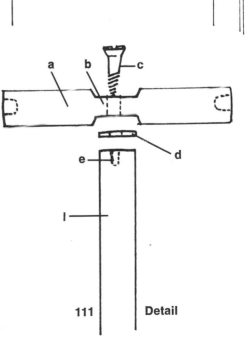

(a) ½" dowel 2¾" long with ¼" hole drilled in each end

(b) ½" long flat space carved in the dowel **(a)** with a knife, with ¼" hole drilled through the flat space. The dowel **(a)** must turn freely on the screw **(c)**.

(c) smooth-shank ⅜₆" wood screw about ½" long

(d) metal washer

(e) small hole made in the top of the supporting rod **(l)** with an awl. The screw **(c)** fits snugly into this hole.

(f) Tinker Toy wheels. They must turn freely on rods **(h)**.

(g) balsa wood propellers 1" x 9" glued into slots in rods **(h)** at 90° angles to wheels

(h) Tinker Toy rods 1¼" long

(i) thumbtack hubcap to keep front propeller wheel on **(h)**

(j) ½" dowel 1½" long with ¼" hole in one end, slot for tail sawed in other end

(k) balsa tail 4" x 15" glued into slot in **(j)**

(l) ½" wood dowel 31¾" long (for the supporting rod)

111   **Detail**

61

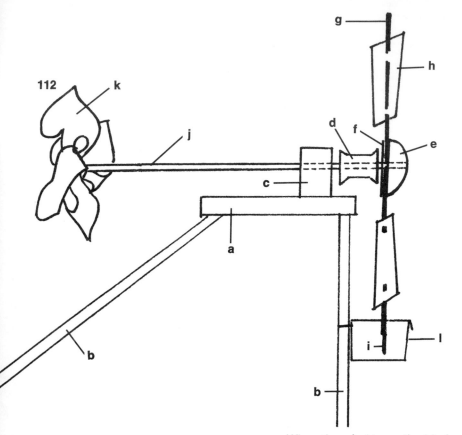

112

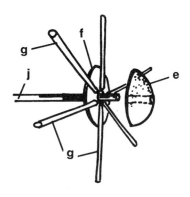

113

When the wind turns the blades of the bubble machine **(112-115)**, rings dip into a tray of liquid soap. The wind blows the bubbles from the rings as they rise from the liquid. The bubble machine must be set up facing the wind. The brass pinwheel spinning behind the machine acts as a balance weight.

You must choose a tray first and build your bubble machine to fit it. The bubbler in the photograph uses a plastic drawer-organizer tray 15″ x 3″ x 2¼″. The diagrams will give you ideas for constructing your bubble machine, but the measurements are based on a 15″ tray only.

(a) scrap wood 1″ x 4½″ x 6½″

(b) 3 wood dowels (only 2 shown here) ½″ x 36″ cut to length you wish for supporting legs

(c) scrap wood (pine) 2" x 2" x 2½" with a ¼" hole drilled through it

(d) large sewing thread spool

(e) half sphere of Styrofoam (or block of wood) hub about 2½" in diameter (or square) with ¼" hole through center. Note: spoked wheel assembly **(e, f, g)** turns freely on rod **(j)**.

(f) stiff cardboard backing to match **(e)**

(g) 6 pieces of ⅛" dowel about 8" long (to make spokes, including the bubble rings **(i)**, two-thirds as long as the tray). Spokes are glued between the hub **(e)** and the backing **(f)**.

(h) 6 blades (about 1½" x 5") of stiff paper (school or file folders) spray-painted with enamel to make them water-resistant. Spokes **(g)** slide through slots cut near each end of blades **(115)**. Arrange all blades at 90° angles to **(e)** and **(f)** so the wind will turn them. Three blades are glued to spokes, and three are left unglued so they can be removed for strong winds.

(i) 3 plastic bubble rings from bubble soap containers glued and taped to 3 spokes **(g)**. From hub to tip, the spokes plus bubble rings measure 9½" long.

(j) small hollow curtain rod (or wood dowel) ¼" x 20"

(k) sheet brass (or stiff paper) pin-wheel (see pinwheel patterns, page 59). In order to catch the wind, the pinwheel must face the machine. If **(j)** is a curtain rod, use a ⅜" dowel about 4" long for the pinwheel axle. Insert the axle in the curtain rod and pinch the rod tight around it with pliers. If **(j)** is a wood dowel, push it through the pinwheel holes as an axle. (Make these pinwheel holes with a paper punch.) A thumbtack in the end of the dowel keeps the pinwheel on.

(l) plastic drawer-organizer tray 15" x 3" x 2¼" with two ⅛" holes drilled near the top for wiring the tray to the front legs **(b)**

(m) arc made by blades with bubble rings (must fit tray)

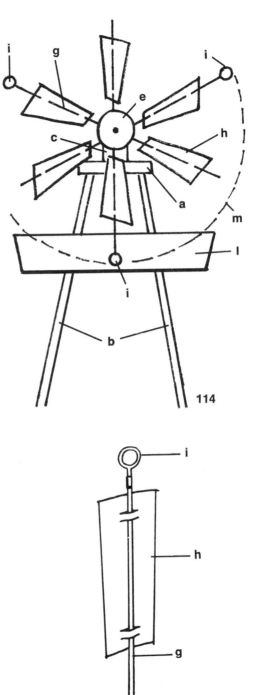

114

115

63

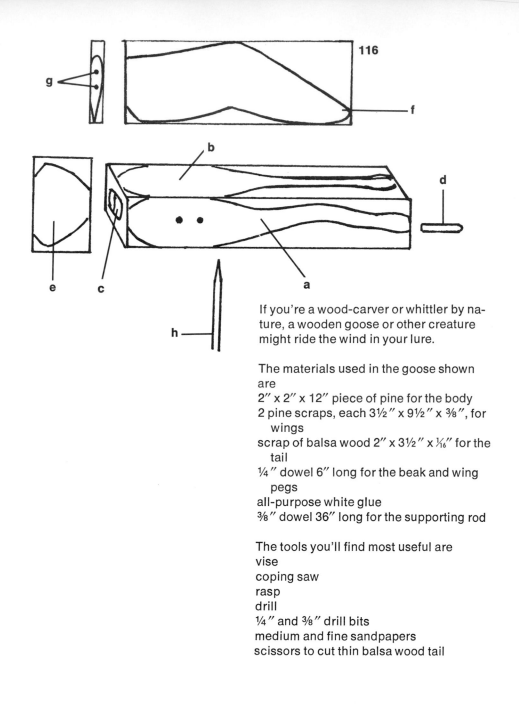

If you're a wood-carver or whittler by nature, a wooden goose or other creature might ride the wind in your lure.

The materials used in the goose shown are
2″ x 2″ x 12″ piece of pine for the body
2 pine scraps, each 3½″ x 9½″ x ⅜″, for wings
scrap of balsa wood 2″ x 3½″ x 1/16″ for the tail
¼″ dowel 6″ long for the beak and wing pegs
all-purpose white glue
⅜″ dowel 36″ long for the supporting rod

The tools you'll find most useful are
vise
coping saw
rasp
drill
¼″ and ⅜″ drill bits
medium and fine sandpapers
scissors to cut thin balsa wood tail

Here are the parts of the carved goose wind finder **(116)**.

(a) body side with holes to match wing holes **(g)**

(b) body top

(c) body back with vertical slot cut in it for tail

(d) beak (for beak hole in head—body front)

(e) tail

(f) wing

(g) end view of wing with holes for pegs (pegs not shown)

(h) ⅜″ supporting dowel for hole in underside of body (hole not shown)

Draw the top, side, and end views of the body on the wood and cut out the drawn shapes with a coping saw.

Use a rasp to define the shape of the body further. Finish with medium and fine sandpapers. For extra smoothness, dampen the wood with a wet rag to raise the grain before the last sanding.

Make the wings by the same method, being careful to make one *right* wing and one *left* wing. The undersides of the wings should be flatter than the top sides.

The wings are mounted on the body with pegs and all-purpose glue. Drill two ¼″ holes at a slight angle downward in each side of the body where the wings will be mounted. The wings will have a slight upward angle when mounted. Drill two matching holes straight into the body end of each wing.

Cut four 1″-long pegs from the ¼″ dowel and *temporarily* attach the wings to mark the balance point for the support hole on the underside of the body. Remove the wings and drill the support hole.

Drill a beak hole in the front end of the body and cut a vertical tail slot in the back end. Cut a 1¼″-long beak and sand it to a gentle taper. Glue the beak into the beak hole. Cut a tail from balsa wood and glue it into the tail slot. Glue on the wings and allow to dry overnight.

Balance the goose on a sharpened wood dowel that fits in the hole on the underside of the body. Its vertical tail will turn it toward the wind.

One wind toy will give you an idea for another, and that for another, until you have designed a great lure of flaps, flutters, chimes, and rattles sure to entice the wind—and attract a few people, too. Everyone likes to watch a spellbound wind.

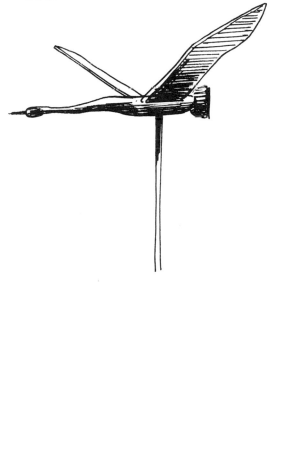

Sources for Materials

Metal kitchen molds—housewares departments, hardware and variety stores, gourmet cooking supply shops

Sheet brass—hobby and craft shops, hardware stores

Wood dowels—hobby shops, hardware and lumber stores

Scrap wood—scrap bins at lumber-yards and small woodworking factories, such as custom furniture shops; discards from stores that receive crated items; or ask local junior high school and high school shop teachers for sources

Bicycle spokes and spoke nipples—an old bicycle wheel, bicycle repair shops

Plastic drawer-organizer tray—housewares departments in variety, drug, hardware, grocery, and department stores

Liquid bubble soap—toy departments in variety, drug, grocery, and discount department stores

Styrofoam sphere or half-sphere—hobby and craft shops, arts and crafts departments, variety stores

Curtain rods—ask friends, landlords, family for discards; housewares departments; variety and hardware stores

Bits and Pieces

Six

A good giant and his good-giantess wife lived on a high mountain over-looking a little village. They had no children of their own but enjoyed watching the children of mortals at play. They often tiptoed to the edge of their realm and lay on their stomachs for hours to watch the children in the valley below.

While tending his goats, the good giant often found colorful or shiny little things, which he saved in a large clay pot by the hearth. Then, on par-ticularly gloomy days, the giantess would sprinkle a few of these bright bits over the village for the children to find. She loved to make them happy.

One day as the giantess was sweeping, she accidentally tipped the pot and set it spinning. It teetered, then rolled out the door—and with the giantess shuffling after it, the pot headed right for the quiet little village. The pot picked up speed as it tumbled along, hitting every pothole on the path until it finally burst into the air in a million pieces.

It rained beautiful bits and shiny things for hours—all over the village below. The giantess crept to the edge of the mountain and peeked over to see the result of her clumsiness. Tears brimmed her star-bright eyes.

The dazed villagers stumbled about, hands to their faces, crying, "Good gracious!" and, "Such a storm from out of nowhere." Then, looking to the sky, they saw her.

The giantess forced a timid smile and whispered, "It's for the children."

The villagers didn't quite understand, but with a giantess looking down on them, they smiled and nodded a lot. The children seemed to understand and loved all the prettiness at their feet. They made towers and figures and paved the streets with designs and made the village the most beautiful in all the land.

Mosaics

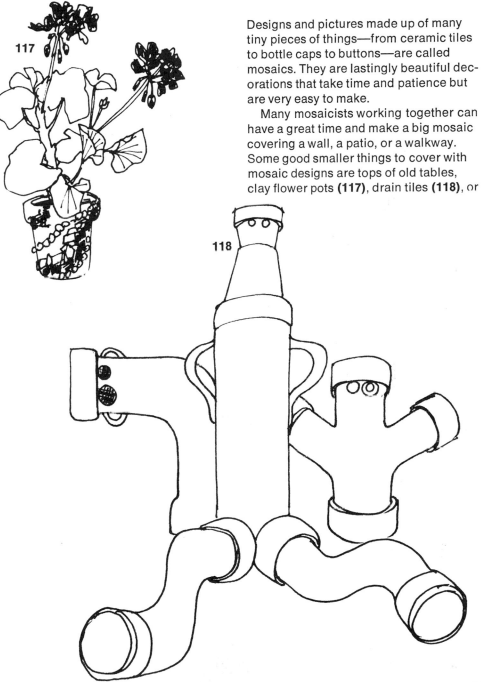

Designs and pictures made up of many tiny pieces of things—from ceramic tiles to bottle caps to buttons—are called mosaics. They are lastingly beautiful decorations that take time and patience but are very easy to make.

Many mosaicists working together can have a great time and make a big mosaic covering a wall, a patio, or a walkway. Some good smaller things to cover with mosaic designs are tops of old tables, clay flower pots **(117)**, drain tiles **(118)**, or

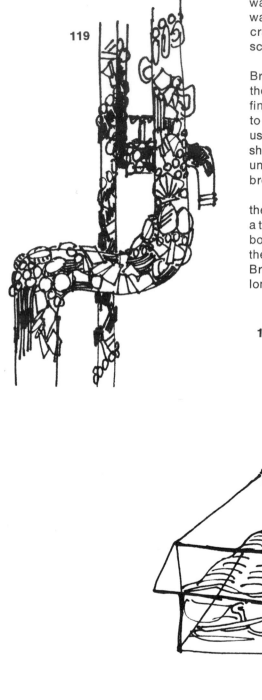

119

water pipes **(119)**, pieces of wood and wallboard, and great-shaped junk such as crankshafts (for fantastic-looking outdoor sculpture).

Bright bits and pieces may not fall out of the sky for you, but children are the best finders there are. So if you set your mind to it, you can collect lots of little things to use in mosaics—things such as pebbles, shells, bottle caps, keys, marbles, and unwanted china and pottery dishes to break up into little pieces.

(120) To break the dishes, separate them according to color. Put one group at a time into a plastic pail or a cardboard box with several layers of newspaper over the dishes to keep the chips from flying. Break them with a ball bat or other heavy long board. Don't crush them into sand;

120

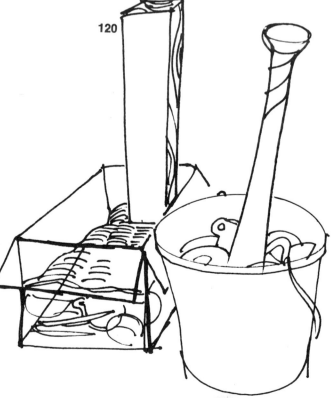

just break them into ½″ to 2″ pieces.
Keep the broken pieces, grouped by color,
in separate small boxes.

Small ceramic tiles are nice to use,
either as accents or by themselves.

Colored glass jars and bottles and little
mirrors are brilliant accents in a mosaic.
*But breaking and handling glass (and
mirrors) is very dangerous and should be
done only by teen-agers or adult helpers.*

(121) Nippers are a great help to a mo-
saicist. They are made especially for
mosaic tile but work beautifully to cut
pieces of china and pottery to fit where
they are needed. A pair of nippers costs
about five dollars but will be useful for
many years of mosaicking.

Making a mosaic is very simple. You need
a clean, dry surface to cover with a mosaic design, the bits and pieces you've
collected, and all-purpose white glue.
Cement (sand mix) is used instead of glue
for patios or walks, and spackling paste
is good for bits and pieces that do not
glue well, such as bottle caps, marbles,
shells, and very curved pottery pieces.
After it is dry, spackling paste must be
sealed from moisture with acrylic spray.

121

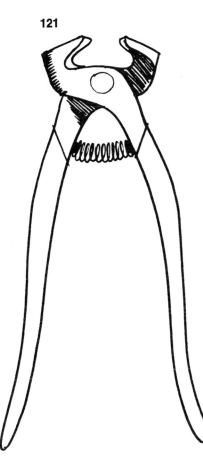

You may draw your design very simply on the working surface, or just think it out as you do the mosaic (122, 123). Working out the details and patterns first, spread

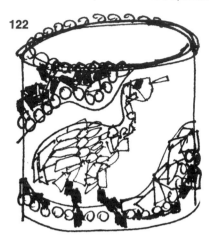

122

glue heavily in one small area at a time and fit the bits and pieces together to make your design or picture. Try to fit the pieces closely together, then fill in the little spaces later with small chips of the right color for the area.

If you don't have enough pieces of a particular color, try painting that area of the working surface with acrylic or enamel paint. A flat painted surface makes a nice area of contrast in a mosaic.

Keep the designs *simple* and step back from your work often to see all the pieces blending together.

Sources for Materials

Clay drain tiles—plumbing and builders' supply stores, garden supply shops, discards at building sites (ask the job foreman)

Old dishes—resale shops, garage and rummage sales, friends, and family

Small ceramic tiles—builders' supply stores, some craft shops, or mail-order craft supply houses (see below)

All-purpose white glue—artists' supply, office supply, hardware, drug, and variety stores; craft and hobby shops

Nippers—some craft shops, mail-order craft supply houses (see below)

Sand mix—hardware and builders' supply stores

Spackling paste—same as for Sand mix

Acrylic spray—hardware, artists' supply, or paint stores; paint and art supply departments; craft and hobby shops

Enamel paint—same as for Acrylic spray

Mail-order supply houses—
Sax Arts and Crafts
207 North Milwaukee Street
Milwaukee, Wisconsin 53202

CCM Arts and Crafts, Inc.
9520 Baltimore Avenue
College Park, Maryland 20740

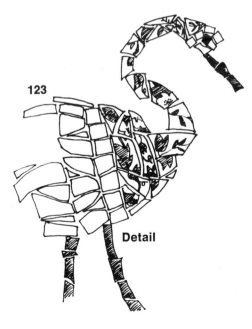

123

Detail

Heartbeats and Drumbeats and Tunes on a Pipe

Seven

Very long ago a young shepherd and his two younger brothers left their village for the first time to take their sheep to greener grasses. They followed the flock through a dense woods to a meadow where the grass was lush and rich with sweet clovers, wild berries, and larks' songs. The flock was content in the sunlit meadow, and so were the young shepherds.

But shadows gathered early, and soon ominous night filled the meadow. The woods crept closer and hid shadowy, nameless things. The shepherds huddled in their blankets, wide-eyed and silent, listening to the darkness. A lone owl hooted, and the rapid, metallic clicking of cricket frogs raced with the shepherds' heartbeats.

"I'm scared," whispered the youngest boy.

"That's silly," scoffed the eldest. "There's nothing out there but our sheep." And swallowing his own fear, he whistled a fragile tune. So the younger boys whistled too, and made rhythms with rocks and sticks and a cooking pot, and felt much braver. A mockingbird made music of their sounds. The wind played on the trees; the pines hummed one tone, the buckthorns another. And the shepherds heard the meadow's night-hidden beauty.

The sweet morning brought thrushes and larks and strange new sounds from the shepherds: rattles, thrums, trills blown through reeds. They invented musical instruments, each more unusual than the one before.

That night a dreadful sound broke from the woods: "Owoul!" The biggest gray wolf they had ever seen sauntered into the moonlit clearing, his shaggy fur rippling like quicksilver. The shepherds went stiff and hollow as dead trees as the wolf waded through the moving sea of sheep.

"Rowl! Shepherds, you make fine music," he said, grinning. "It makes me feel good all over." He did a little shuffle. Noticing the shepherds' wooden stares, he tried his most convincing voice: "Now don't worry about your sheep. I don't even like the taste of sheep. Besides, the fleece sticks to the roof of my mouth and the horns are a bother. I only steal sheep when I haven't anything better to do." He plucked a stringed instrument with his nail, and his hairs twitched. "I wouldn't touch your sheep tonight if you could think of something better for me to do," he hinted, giving the string another pluck.

It's risky business to make a deal with a wolf, but the shepherd, to his brothers' horror, suggested the wolf join them in their music-making. "Here, wolf, you may play the most important instrument of all."

"This one, with all the strings?" asked the wolf, eagerly wiping his hand-paws on his chest. He plucked the strings and gave a little sigh. "Music does something to me," he confided.

"I hope so," muttered the shepherd (so only his brothers could hear). Then, playing a monotonous drum, a three-tone pipe, and a moaning musical bow, the shepherds began. The wolf played enthusiastically, bobbing his head to the beat, and howling under his breath.

With dreamy eyes and his lips pursed with pleasure, the wolf played louder and louder. The boys watched him closely. Then, drumming all the while, and piping sweetly, the shepherds slipped away and herded their flock right out of the musical meadow as quietly as the moon itself.

The boys told their story to all the shepherds of the village, and the story spread to all the shepherds (and wolves) throughout the land—to the wolves' great embarrassment.

Since that time shepherds have played music on their lonely night watches as a reminder to wolves—a disturbing reminder of the powers of music in the hands of the clever.

Musical Instruments

Since sound is made by vibrations, a musical instrument must have something to vibrate and a sound box, or resonator, to make the sound last longer. The bigger the sound box, the more resonance the tones have (the longer the sound lasts).

In a simple musical bow made by primitive people **(124)**, the plucked string vibrates and the coconut-shell cup on the bow is the sound box.

A long string makes a low-pitched tone when plucked. The shorter the string, the higher the pitch. When several strings are all the same length on an instrument, different pitches are made by using strings of different thicknesses and by varying the degree of tautness of each string. The thicker and looser the string, the lower the pitch; the thinner and tighter the string, the higher the pitch.

124

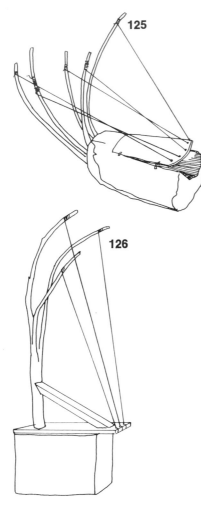

125

126

The three-string "bass branch-harp" in the photograph is a variation of the musical bow and similar to an African harp called a *nanga* **(125)** made of strings of different lengths stretched from sticks to a hollow log.

You can make a bass branch-harp **(126)** with strings of nylon macramé cord stretched taut between tree branches and a wood base glued with all-purpose white glue to a corrugated cardboard sound box. The overhanging end of the wood base has holes drilled through it for tying on the strings (see knots, pages 49-51). The strings may also be knotted around short sticks or wooden beads and slipped into slots cut in the end of the base **(126a)**, or tied to nails.

The branch is nailed to the wood base from underneath before the sound box is added. A scrap of pine 2" x 4" x 16" with the ends sawed at angles for a better fit braces the branch against the pull of the strings. It is nailed to the branch and the wood base before the sound box is added. Try bass viol, cello, or guitar strings for different sound qualities.

The tin can "wah-wah" **(127)** uses a guitar G string as a vibrator, a coffee can sound box, and a foot pedal board to tighten and loosen the string, changing the pitch as it is plucked. The string is threaded through a hole in the can and a hole in the foot pedal and tied to wooden beads so it won't slip through.

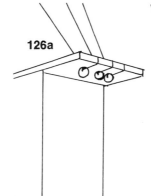

126a

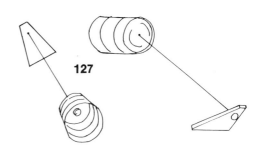

127

The wah-wah is a variation of the musical bow. You can design many more stringed instruments, large and small, based on the wah-wah or the branch bass.

The "fifteen-tone thummer," or thumb piano, uses metal tongues instead of strings. The tongues are of different lengths and vibrate as they are stroked (one or more at a time), making different pitches. Wooden tongues were used in primitive thumb pianos. The tongues on the fifteen-tone thummer in the photograph are made of spring steel "bristles" from street sweeper brushes (found along the curbs wherever street sweepers travel). They are flat, about 9″ long and ⅛″ wide. The length of the tongues from the front tip to the metal bridge is what determines the pitch of each tongue. By sliding the tongues forward or backward, the thummer can be retuned to make different pitches.

A thumb piano **(128, 129)** may be any size or shape and may have any number of tongues. This one **(129)** is 12″ square and 6″ deep and is made of pine and ¼″ plywood. The tongues are held in place on the sound box by the anchor rod **(c)**, which presses them downward, bending them between two bridges. Bridge **(a)** and anchor rod **(c)** are metal for good, clear sound **(130)**. The back bridge **(b)** is wood. It holds the tongues off the box to prevent rattle. Any wood or metal rods or strips may be used for the bridges. Here bridge **(a)** and anchor rod **(c)** happen to be metal wall brackets for shelving. They already had holes in them, so were cut with a hacksaw to fit the sound box and screwed into place. The back bridge **(b)** is a strip of wood molding, nailed to the box. You might use metal rods and a wood dowel **(131)** and tie them to the box through tiny holes drilled in it.

128

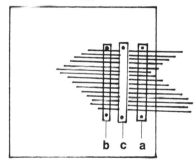

129

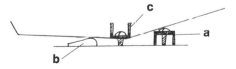

130

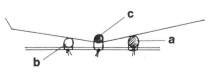

131

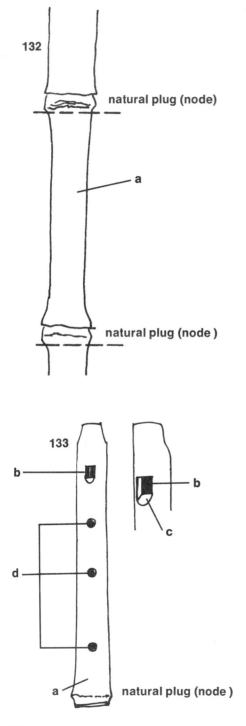

132

natural plug (node)

a

natural plug (node)

133

b

b

c

d

a   natural plug (node)

A shepherds' pipe is a tricky thing to make. You might get lucky on the first try, but more likely you'll make two or three before you are completely satisfied.

The air blown into a pipe travels through a mouthpiece, which in one way or another makes the air vibrate and become a sound wave. The hollow tube of the pipe is the resonator or sound box. A short, small-diameter pipe makes high-pitched tones. A long, large-diameter pipe makes low-pitched tones.

The pipe in the photograph is only 6½″ long, but toots sweetly. A pipe this short must have the lower end plugged to double the distance the sound waves travel. A shorter distance makes a higher pitch, and in this pipe, if the end were open, the pitch would be so high that human ears could not hear it. A 10″ or 12″ pipe may have an open end.

There are no rules as to how many finger holes there should be. One hole makes a two-tone pipe—one tone when blown with the hole open, another with the hole closed. Finger holes drilled about 1⅛″ or farther apart make a noticeable difference in pitch on a small pipe.

Bamboo is a good wood for a pipe, since it is already hollow and has a natural plug at each bump or node. If possible, start with a long piece of bamboo and saw just below the bumps or nodes **(132)** to make several shorter pieces to work with.

The best tools for making this pipe are:

coping saw   ³⁄₁₆″ and ¼″ drill bits
vise   small knife
drill

These diagrams show how the pipe in the photograph was made.
(132, 133)

(a) A bamboo section cut below the natural plugs (nodes). To shape the mouthpiece, saw the hollow end at an angle as shown in **(135b)**.

(b) Window—about ¼″ square on a thin pipe. Start with a ¼″ drilled hole and carve the square edges and window sill **(c)** with an X-acto or other small knife.

    (c) Window sill—must be cut at an angle (about 45°) as shown.

    (d) Finger holes drilled with a ³⁄₁₆″ drill bit—second hole 1⅛″ below first, third hole 1¾″ below second.

    (134) Finished mouthpiece (seen from the end) with plug in place. The plug is carved from a fresh willow or other twig with the bark peeled off. Fresh twigs are moist and work better than dry woods.

    (135) Shape of the mouthpiece plug before the end is trimmed to match the pipe mouthpiece. You may have to carve a few plugs before one fits snugly and angles correctly inside the bamboo pipe.

    (135a) Angle of the mouthpiece plug inside the pipe. The lower end must line up with the inside edge of the window sill. The air you blow into the pipe is guided by the angle of the plug to touch the inside edge of the window sill. That edge disturbs the air and starts a vibration, or sound wave, traveling through the pipe. Try making sounds to check the angle before the plug is glued in place.

    (135b) Glue the mouthpiece plug in place with all-purpose white glue before trimming the mouth end. When the glue is dry, use a coping saw to trim the plug end to match the pipe mouthpiece.

Very young shepherds (and other people) can have a lot of fun rediscovering what is probably the history of musical instruments. Try making notched-stick scrapers **(136)**, old wooden bowl clappers **(137)**, drums from all sorts of things **(138)**, gong chimes **(139)**, xylophones from different

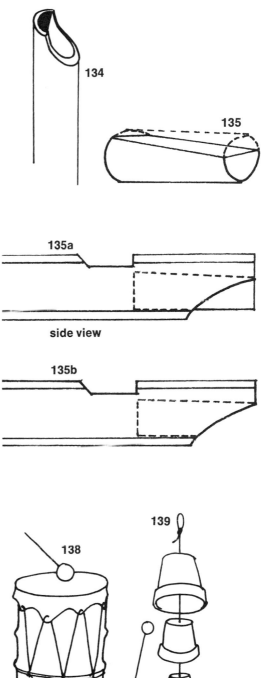

side view

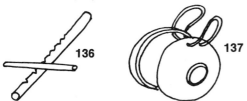

lengths of metal pipes or even cardboard tubes **(140)**, sand-blocks **(141)**, and many more musical sound-makers of your own design.

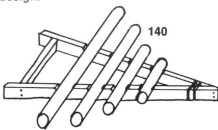

140

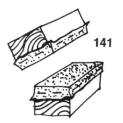

141

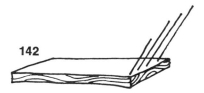

142

143

(142) You might try a variation of the thumb piano by sticking metal knitting needles (with the heads removed) into a piece of wood. Sit on one end of it on a hollow porch or fire escape and the whole porch becomes the sound box. Or hold it against a shed or panel truck or any big, hollow thing you can find.

(143) For a real musical surprise, listen to an oven rack hanging from a cord. Wrap the ends of the cord around your index fingers and put your fingers in your ears. Bend over so the oven rack hangs freely and have a friend strum the rack with a pencil or fork or something made of plastic.

Music is best when you are making it. There are no rules. If it sounds musical to you, it's music.

Sources for Materials

Nylon cord—craft and some yarn shops, hardware stores, marine supply stores

Bass viol, cello, and guitar strings—music stores, discards from musical instrument repair shops, and music teachers and friends who play these instruments

Metal rods—hardware and hobby stores, builders' supply stores

Spring steel (flat spring steel wire)—grass rake prongs, clock and watch repair shops, hardware stores; or ask junior high school and high school metal shop teachers for sources

X-acto knife—hobby and craft stores, artists' supply and hardware stores

Wooden beads—toy departments, variety stores, craft and hobby shops

Bamboo—garden supply stores, discount department stores, and fishing poles from sporting goods departments

All-purpose white glue—artists' supply, office supply, hardware, drug, and variety stores; craft and hobby shops

Mud Myra

Eight

Very soon now, if you haven't already done so, you'll find an irresistible mixture of water and dirt and meet Myra (the wonderful), spirit of mud. She will lure you from the dry rim of a mud puddle into the most squishy center before you know what's happening. You'll surrender without a struggle to this old, dear spirit, for she's as ancient as mud itself and knows all the ways to be attractive.

Mysteriously, she'll smudge you with muddy stripes and spots, marking you as hers on your first day with her; and you won't feel a thing except excitement. You'll suddenly dip both hands into her mud puddle for no reason you can think of—that's the sign that you are Myra's (for a while).

Myra has seen the mud marvels of the world—aborigines coated with mud for their ritual dances; ovenbirds' and barn swallows' nests made of mud and straw like the adobe bricks of Indian pueblos; the mud pots of the remarkable potter wasps and Indian bowls, both decorated with patterns of different colored muds. And now Mud Myra is about to see the beauties of your mud art.

She'll coax you to her mud puddle and invite you to leave your mark. Make it beautiful. Build her a monument etched with patterns, imprinted with designs. Dig canyons and caves and marvelous tunnels. Make a mud garden paved with pebbles and marbles, planted with drizzled spires and satiny mounds. Give in to your whims, and the old genius herself will urge you on.

Mud Art

Good mud to work with is not sandy but very much like potters' clay. The more clay there is in the mud, the better it is for modeling. If your mud is visited by a yellow-legged mud dauber wasp **(144)**, you can be sure you have great mud. She is a mud expert and chooses only the best for her nest of tubular cells. Leave her undisturbed and she won't bother you at all.

You may find large clay deposits in your mud. The clay sticks together, is of a slightly different color from the mud, and feels a little gummy. The mud rinses away easily, so you can collect a handful or so of pure clay and make a little pot or figure from it.

Most mud can be squeezed and patted into shapes, imprinted, scratched, or smoothed to a satiny sheen. It can be thinned with water and smeared or brushed onto a surface such as a wall and raked with patterns. So take a few tools besides hands and feet to the mud **(145–152)**.

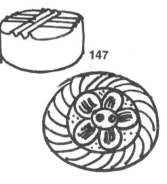

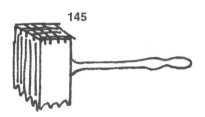

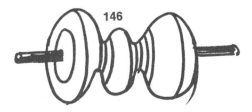

149

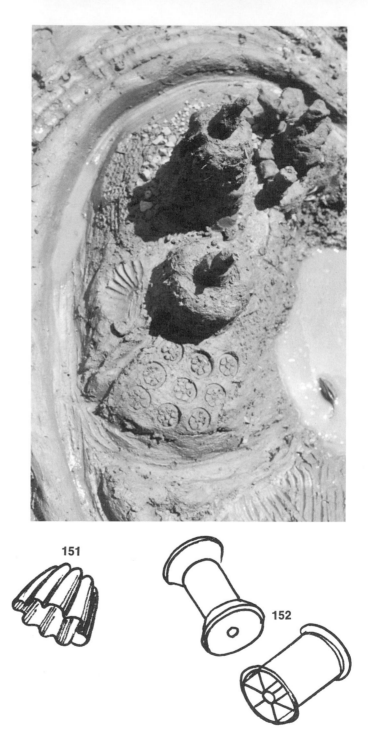

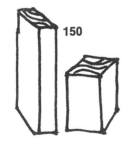

150

151

152

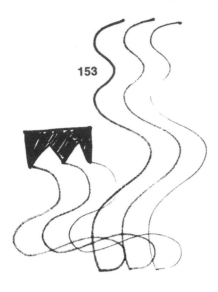

Try imprints of everything from buttons to door knobs to bicycle tires—spools, cooking molds, forks, spoons, a meat pounder, a potato masher, tin cans (with air-escape holes in the tops), turned wood pieces, and wood blocks.

(153) For scraping patterns on a mud-washed wall, use twigs or make rakes from stiff cardboard.

Try making bricks to build with—small ones made in ice cube trays or large ones made in bread pans and dried in the sun. Mud mixed with dead grass clippings makes strong bricks similar to adobe.

It's no use trying to stay neat around mud, so wear old clothes and really get into your work. Have a garden hose or a pail of water handy to rinse off your hands for a fresh start once in a while and to make soupy mud when you want it.

When you leave Mud Myra, be considerate—wash yourself off *before* you go inside.

"I guess they're my feet, but they don't look like the ones I had on this morning."

The Snow Beast and
The Crystal Castle

Nine

(A STORY IN TWO PARTS)

Part One: The Snow Beast

Frost ferns grow flat against the windows as if winter were trying to make itself as pretty as possible. Flakes aswirl in the drab sky have the whole quiet world to themselves. The sky looks mean and creeps closer. Only the spiky skeletons of summer's trees hold it back. The wind hurls a few flakes at the windows—the signal that a spectacle is about to begin. The children know: a snow beast is coming at last.

Wherever there are children and real winters, the snow beast is likely to appear. Too heavy to come crashing down all at once, he rides the wind to a likely place, then scatters himself over the earth. For those few joyful moments, he is more delicate than butterflies. He would fly forever if he could. How he envies wispy-winged summer creatures and fairies—the fairies most of all; the sneaky fairies with their hidden treasures and secrets and snug little sunlit castles where they hide stolen bits of summer.

A snow beast tries to fall in a place where children will find him and help him get himself together for his own very special winter game.

The children know what has to be done and are ready long before the last dizzy flakes settle. Sleds and snow shovels slide into action, moving the white stuff of the great beast to the place chosen for his reunion. They are anxious to see what he'll look like, for he's never the same beast twice. He may become a lovely snow queen, a lizard-beast, a giant crab, or a nameless monstrosity of lumps with many eyes and great claws. Each time he comes, he takes a different form. It's part of his plan.

The children pile and poke and smooth the snow, and the beast reveals himself to them slowly. He is rather gross, but not without his likeable side, and the children admire him. The younger ones stand at a respectful distance and smile.

Snow Sculpture

Dry, powdery snow is beautiful, but it's not the stuff of the snow beast. He comes down wet and heavy and perfect for packing.

Unless you're lucky enough to have a deep snowfall, you must scoop your snow beast from here and there onto sleds and move as much of him to one place as you can. Tie a cardboard carton to your sled so you can haul more snow with each trip. A snow shovel (or two or three, and friends to use them) is a big help.

(154-161) As you mound the snow and pack it hard, the beast will appear, part by part. Your ideas of what he's beginning to look like will play an important part in his creation.

Waterproof gloves or mittens pack snow better than knitted ones. If all you have are knitted mitts, wear plastic bags (such as bread bags) over your mittens with rubber bands at the wrists to keep them on. The plastic smooths the snow beautifully, keeps your hands dry and warmer, and will leave wrinkle prints in patted snow—a nice touch for a beast.

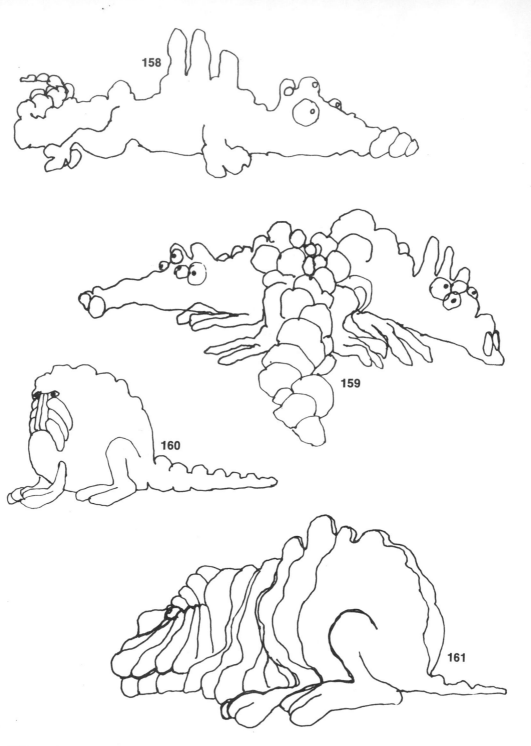

158

159

160

161

Part Two: The Crystal Castle

It is said that a band of wealthy fairies often hides its palace in a woodsy place near the sweet scent of evergreens. Having used all sorts of trickery to gather their wealth, the fairies are quite smug and obnoxious about it and guard it jealously. They like their secrets and, above all, they do not like to be seen.

Throughout the warmer months the fairies' castle was as invisible as they themselves. But winter has stilled the world. Its cold, wet breath has iced the delicate walls and spires and glimmering gewgaws of their secret place. Gateways and turrets are frosted and the rainbows frozen in their towers for all to see.

The terrible snow beast must surely be near. The fairies fly in every direction, doing what mischief they can to divert attention from their castle. They must be alert and more clever than ever, for only the warming sun will make their treasure safely invisible again.

Under cover of night the snow beast moves as quietly as his own shadow, unnoticed even by the moon. Driven on by the faint scent of evergreen and the sound of music so fragile, he searches.

As dawn slides over the horizon, the winter sun rolls upward. The snow beast feels uneasy with the sudden stinging warmth at his back. He crouches closer to the cold ground, knowing his time is short. Then a sliver of dim sunlight touches what seems to be a row of gleaming diamonds. It slips through the evergreens, taps a silver spire, and sets it ringing.

The fairies fly into a twitter, frantic at the sight of the great indelicate hulk crouched before them, staring. They hurl themselves at him—an invisible whirlwind of wings. It is no use. He drives them wild with his eyes—and loves every minute of it. The snow beast has won. A smug grin cracks across his face. Even as he softens, he stares at their crystal halls and domes of morning light—and at their rainbow tower. He has never before seen a rainbow.

Ice Molds

A glimmering crystal castle is a fanciful arrangement of curious shapes made (by mortals such as you and me) in molds filled with water and frozen. If the weather stays cold, an ice castle will last for many days, then slowly disappear—as one might expect of a fairy castle.

162

163

Molds for ice making must be plastic, rubber, or metal—*not glass*. When water freezes, it expands, pushing outward in all directions. Under that pressure, glass breaks. The molds must be straight-sided, or larger at the top than at the bottom so the ice can be removed.

Here is a sampling of some known castle parts and molds you might use to duplicate them.

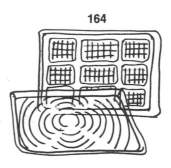

164

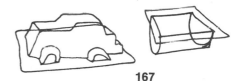

166

(162) Solid domes and thin bowl-domes (stacked plastic bowls with water in both bowls)

(163) Thin discs (plastic lids)

(164) Fancy walls and roofs of patterned sheets of ice (plastic meat trays with ridged patterns—from supermarkets)

(165) Cones with spires (funnels with small ends plugged—gum or a potato makes a good plug)

(166) Tall spire (baster with rubber ball end removed and small end plugged)

(167) Mysterious shapes that look almost familiar (assorted clear plastic coverings from toy packaging)

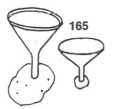

165

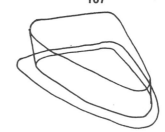

167

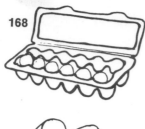
168

(168) Small half-domes (plastic Easter egg halves or styrene egg cartons)

(169) Bricks for walls and foundations (good old ice cube trays)

(170) Tiny knobs (fancy new ice cube trays)

(171) Fancy patterned shapes (various molds from the kitchen)

(172) Thick discs (cupcake pans)

(173) Giant hand for a gate, a bridge, or a courtyard sculpture (a rubber glove)

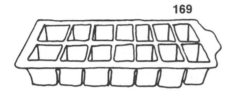
169

Note: *Do not handle freezing-cold metal molds without gloves or plastic bags over your hands, for the metal will freeze to your skin and hurt you terribly.*

170

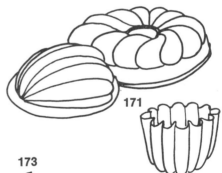
171

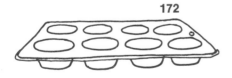
172

173

Set your fanciful molds outside in freezing weather and fill them with water. Add a few drops of food coloring and watch it swirl. It will freeze in swirls if the water is very cold first. You might add a sprig of something pretty with berries on it, marbles, or little trinkets for color. Leave the filled molds undisturbed overnight or until the water is frozen solid.

Choose a site for your crystal castle that is mostly shady but has some sunlight to highlight the palace with sparkles.

The air temperature must be freezing (32° F) or below when you construct your ice castle. Dip the molds into a pail of warm water for three or four seconds or until the ice shapes slide easily from the molds. Do not bang the molds to release the ice, for ice is very brittle by the nature of the crystal formations that make it.

Use a plastic spray-bottle of water to freeze-weld the ice pieces together. A little snow is a great help in holding your first ice walls in position, but if there is no snow, spray the ground and the edges to be joined and hold the pieces in place on the wet surface until they freeze together. Add one castle piece at a time, spraying the surfaces to be joined, and holding the pieces until they stick together—a few seconds.

(174-176) As a final touch for your castle, go icicle hunting for some tall spires or an icicle gate.

174

175